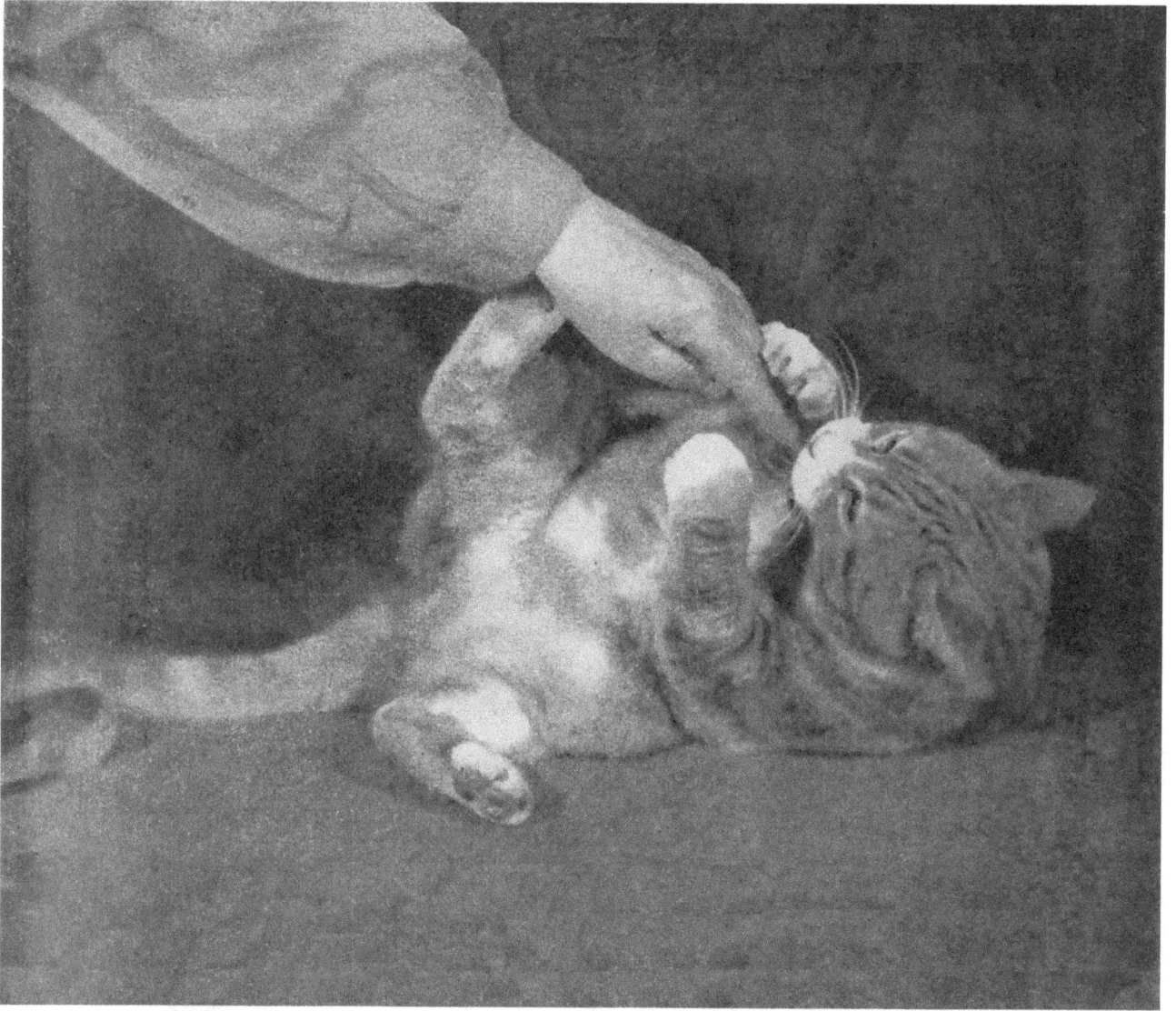

Ginger

Courtyard of Ola's Home

MOSTLY CATS

BY
OLA COHN A.R.C.A. (LONDON)

AUTHOR OF
"THE FAIRIES' TREE"
"MORE ABOUT THE FAIRIES' TREE"
AND
"CASTLES IN THE AIR"

Published by Robert W Strugnell (Melbourne)
www.fitzroygardens.com

First Published 2017

ISBN 978-0-9954330-1-4

National Library of Australia Cataloguing-in-Publication entry

Creator: Cohn, Ola, 1892-1964, author.

Title: Mostly Cats / Ola Cohn.

ISBN: 9780995433014 (paperback)

Subjects: Cohn, Ola, 1892-1964.
Sculptors—Victoria—Biography.
Women artists—Victoria—Biography.
Artists—Victoria—20th century—Biography.
Art, Australian—20th century—History.

I HAVE WRITTEN THIS BOOK FOR
THE SHEER LOVE OF MY FELLOW
CREATURES, AND I DEDICATE IT TO
MY DEAR FRIEND AND FELLOW
ARTIST
MARJORIE McCHESNEY MATHEWS
WHO SHARES THIS LOVE.
OLA.

Melbourne, May 1964.

CONTENTS

ILLUSTRATIONS

FOREWORD

This book is a fulfilment of a long cherished desire to record the delightful memories of my contact with Australian Fauna and particularly my domestic pals, and was inspired by my great love for these dependant animals and the peace and tranquillity associated with my belief in fairies, who have been my constant companions since childhood.

I would be remiss if I did not thank Ada Withers for her help in assisting with the typing of rough manuscripts and to Marjorie McChesney Mathews, to whom I have dedicated this book, for her collaboration in respect to the supervision of the final manuscripts.

O.C.

MY LOVE FOR CREATURES

I was born with a love for creatures and throughout my life that love has never died. The older I become the more sensitive I am to their strange little ways and habits. Being akin, I sometimes wonder whether I am all human and if there is not in my soul the simplicity of their nature. They know this and talk to me in a language I understand. My cats spit when they are annoyed, or feelings hurt, if pleased they purr and rub against my leg as if to say "It's suppertime". When they sit on my window sill, chattering their teeth and gazing intently at an unsuspecting honeyeater feeding from the blossom of a Loquat tree nearby, I know they expect me to open the window so that they can have a nearer view. When they struggle, yell, and refuse to be put into their basket, they do not want to go to the vet. All these little ways they communicate and I understand, and deep down our friendship never falters.

As a child I thought it would not be difficult to tame a snake as all creatures respond to kindness and understanding. These qualities I seem to possess as far as animals are concerned. But I never got an opportunity to tame any wild creatures as most of our pets were domestic. I was particularly fond of cats, and as long as I can remember I have always had one. At one period I had no less than three kittens. These poor little beggars I dressed in dolls' clothes and put to sleep in a pram. I did not have this trio long for when they grew to cats they mysteriously disappeared. I believe father took them to his malt house as there the mice were bad.

CEREMONIAL FUNERALS

Mother having fresh air ideas arranged for my sister Franziska and me to sleep outside on the back verandah, not far from an aviary full of birds. These pretty wee things fluttered about and seemed quite happy in their confined space. In the early morning hours I would sometimes be awakened by strange scratching sounds. Creeping out of bed with my candle held high and my ears alert I followed in the wake of the sound, only to discover a family of mice having a wonderful feed on the birds' seed which was scattered in every corner of the cage. Nothing we could do would keep away the mice and, as they had migrated to the kitchen, mouse-traps were bought and laid in all cupboards. Soon families of them were dead, squashed flat by the cruel wire that had sprung back on them unsuspectedly. Sammie the big Manx ginger cat was given the kill, which he played with for hours. When they had been tossed in the air many times and well chewed, I rescued the sad looking emasculated body and borrowing my brother's toy cart I put the tiny corpse in a box, and surrounded it with flowers and placed it in the make-believe hearse. Dragging it along with a piece of string we performed a ceremonial funeral. Brother Marc followed with a toy shovel. After he had dug a small hole, the coffin was lowered. When it was well covered with earth a tombstone was placed at the head, and after shedding a crocodile tear the ceremony was over.

In this cemetery in the corner of father's garden were buried many unfortunate creatures who had succumbed in our large grounds, and even the burying of a colourful beetle was done with as full honours as that of a mauled mouse.

FIRST OF APRIL

One cold April morning, when I was tucked in my airy bed on the verandah, I heard brother Leo calling from the stables "Come quickly, Sammie has kittens". I jumped out of bed, and without putting on my slippers, ran up to the top yard and almost bounded into the stables. There was Sammie comfortably lying on a half bag of wheat. I walked cautiously up to him but could see no kittens. From over my shoulder I heard Leo call "April Fool; Sammie's a gentleman". I sat down beside my cat feeling cold, disappointed and annoyed. I cried, whilst Sammie purred. As I stroked him tears fell from my eyes, nearly blinding me. With the corner of my nightgown I wiped them away, and, seeing clearly, I noticed movement in a half bag of wheat. It was seething with mice, and my old cat sitting there too lazy to stir! I thought he must be tired, so decided to catch them for him. This was easily done from the outside of the sack and in no time I had captured four. Three I put in a tin for later meals, the fourth I gave to him. Suddenly he woke up and grabbing the poor small creature in cruel teeth ran to the corner of the stable, growling and making a tremendous fuss, and acting as if he had caught it all by himself. I left hurriedly as I could not bear to see the poor creature being tossed about and later killed. I knew Father wanted to get rid of the mice and excused myself by thinking I was only doing my duty. Now I am an adult I will not tolerate mouse-catching other than with a trap, which means a quick death.

I left the stable a little crestfallen, and meeting our nurse, Aggie, was told to wash and dress as breakfast was ready, so, putting the tin containing the mice on the verandah table, I went inside. I had hardly left when Aggie curiously picked it up, opened the lid and out jumped the mice. It gave her such a fright that she ran screaming into the kitchen with her long skirt held high, so I had the satisfaction of not being the only one fooled.

2

THE SORROW OF DEATH

Sammie lived many years a happy lazy life. As he got older he developed sores and my parents thinking him unhealthy to have about, decided it was time for him to pass on, but I would not accept the fact and burst into tears every time it was mentioned. The verdict being given, a big, strong, burly workman came to take him away. With terror grappling at my heart, I grabbed my cat in my arms, and, running up the top yard, locked myself and my cat in the old groom's room in the old stables. Through a wire-netting which had replaced the broken glass of the door, I defied the big burly brute who had come to take away my pet. After much argument through the frail partition, the man left, saying my father would have to deal with the matter. When I was quite sure it was safe, I opened the door and came out. I still had my pet and nursed him more fondly than ever, which upset my parents as Sammie was a sick cat. He was allowed to live on for a while and I rejoiced as I thought they had forgotten their threat, but I was mistaken as their silence was only a bluff. Later, when I was away for a short holiday, Sammie disappeared. I never heard exactly what happened to him; I never wanted to. He had just gone when I got back. I called and hunted for him everywhere, but nowhere could he be found. That night I was told that Sammie had passed on. I went silently to bed with a lump in my throat and a pain in my heart, knowing the sorrow of death for the first time. I could hear Mother singing in the ballroom, and I knew that Father was sitting by the fire listening. She was singing about a goldfish which swam in a big glass bowl. It was a sad song and I cried, and with tears came sleep, and then I was happy for I had found my Sammie in dreamland.

OTHER PETS

I fretted for a long time over the passing of my cat, so Father being soft-hearted, gave me a ginger kitten. He was also a Manx and very like Sammie, but, he never quite took his place in my heart. Billie Muggins, our dog, arrived about the same time. He was not unlike an English Sheepdog. The dog inspector did not know how to classify him as he had no pedigree to go by, and since we could not name his father, the puzzle of his classification remained unsolved.

I HELP MARGOO BUILD A NEST

Margoo, the black backed piping crow (known as the Australian magpie), was given to me when she was quite a young bird. Being very tame and also of the female species, she was a much nicer nature than Margu, my other magpie who came later. He proved by his aggressive ways to be a male. Margoo would sleep on the end of my bed on the verandah and in the morning would gently pull my eyelashes to wake me, and was even familiar enough to snuggle into bed for a cuddle.

In the mating season Margoo became wayward and would wander round the neighbourhood, and I would have to go in search of her. She loved to perch on the branch of a rustic arch in the garden. There she would fluff her feathers and wag her tail, and with her head outstretched, call a beautiful wild note hoping the elements would carry her message to some wild creature of her kind. It was sad to see her craving for a mate to share her love.

One spring day the gods were kind to Margoo. They heard her plaintive voice calling and, taking pity, blew the sound of her craving note to the ears of a wild magpie. He did not delay in answering, but flew straight to the garden, so eager was he for her love. For many weeks he stayed in the garden and, although I tried, I could not make friends with him, he was so timid and shy. But for Margoo he showed great affection, and she accepting his love, wasted no time in preparing a home. I watched her preparation with the greatest of interest and decided that perhaps I could help, so went in search of a pair of pliers. when Margoo found a piece of wire she could not detach from some object, I came to the rescue and snipped it off. Having collected a bundle she would lead me to her nesting place in the garden. I kept on the rear like a flunkey. When we came to her selected pepper-corn tree she hopped up to the top branches, and waited until I had climbed to within a few feet of her, then she asked in a soft squeaky voice for some building material. I passed her a bit at a time and watched her twist the stiff wire into the already formed foundation, and with tugs and pulls she placed every bit to her liking. This procedure went on for days. When she was quite satisfied with the structure she lined her nest with soft feathers from the fowl yard.

During this performance the wild bird kept its distance, but nevertheless watched each step. I suppose he thought me interfering, as I was doing his job, and I must confess that perhaps he was right, for when the offspring was born in the shape of an egg I handled it so much that even Margoo objected and neglected the nest. The egg became cold and nothing happened.

SILKWORM BREEDING

Silkworm breeding was the vogue amongst children and all well conducted families possessed some specimens. Marc first purchased ours for the price of a penny a hundred and resold me a share. These little midgets, with their soft white skins and black noses, I placed in a box full of mulberry leaves. They are greedy things and never stop eating, nibbling away leaves so quickly that in no time large slices were devoured. As the worms grow fat and big they become lazy and gradually stop eating. At this stage of their existence they become stationary and, like white marble statues, they stay with raised heads as if in a trance. After some time they gradually become alive again and making their way to a corner of their box start weaving a beautiful cocoon. Before the worm is allowed to proceed far with his house-building, he is picked out of his box and placed in a cornucopia paper bag, which is pinned to the wall. In this convenient shape it weaves its secluded home. The first threads are loosely spun, then gradually they are drawn tighter and tighter. Working from the inside, they are eventually covered with a firm egg shape of silk. There they stay until they change from a worm to a chrysalis. Then the exciting part begins; winding of the silk from the cocoon. When the right thread is discovered, it is wound round a piece of cardboard with a long old-fashioned hat pin stuck through the middle, which acts as an axle. Twisting this with the fingers one soon has a fine skein of silk. When the chrysalis is exposed it is placed in a box full of nice soft bran and there stay until it emerges as a beautiful white moth. Then the winged creature immediately breeds. The result is hundreds of eggs! And the next year hundreds and hundreds of worms! Then one is glad to give them away to anyone who will bother with their cultivation.

As I slept out-of-doors, the main space in my bedroom was fairly clear of furniture. This was a grand place to keep my many boxes of worms, which were at this time big and had reached the lazy stage. I tended these creatures with great care, always seeing that they were well supplied with plenty of fresh leaves and that their boxes were kept clean. They were my main source of interest over a long period, so imagine my dismay when entering my room one morning to find dead worms strewn all over the floor and a large rat hole nibbled in the skirting board. I was most distressed at the wholesale slaughter and decided that I must take precautions so that it would not occur again. That night, when retiring, I stuffed the toe of my shoe in the hole to act as a cork; then went to bed and slept soundly. In the morning I was horrified to find disorder in my room again. Leaves were dragged from the boxes and the corpses of half-eaten worms lay in ghastly postures in all directions. My shoe was still wedged in the hole and, although I pried into all the corners of the room, I could not see any obvious clue as to where the murderers had entered. After searching for a while I gave up and dressed. Extracting my shoe from the hole, so that I could wear it to school, I was astonished to see that the whole of the toe was eaten away. I was upset because I thought mother would be cross but to my surprise she was amused. The joke was on me, but for the worms a complete tragedy.

THE BUNGALOW

For twenty-three years we lived in our bungalow home in Bendigo. They were the happiest days of my life. There I laughed, cried and played. When I look back on those years they seem but yesterday and I often wish I could live them again.

The house was large and rambling, and almost completely surrounded by verandahs, with many turns and corners. In one section, overlooking the garden, we often sat on hot summer evenings, breathing in the perfume from the flowers and listening to Mother tell of the mysteries of "The Bungalow", how it once stood in Pall Mall beside the Bendigo Creek. It was originally the Post Office, but when the new building was erected, the old place was put up for sale. It was soon purchased and as the land on which it stood had become so valuable the house was moved and rebuilt in Barkly Place. The stones were three foot through and were all marked before demolition. The owner added a wing, which included a ballroom. In front of the house, in the centre of the gable, there was a hole where the Post Office clock used to be. It is now covered with wire and a paradise for spiders.

SECRET STAIRCASE

A secret staircase embedded in the wall between the big lounge with its three large French-windows, and Sister Lorna's bedroom, was a great mystery to us, and part of "The Bungalow's" charm. The lounge had been the old Post Office's sorting room and, as valuable packages and letters were passing through in the gold-rush days, many thefts were happening. It had not been safe to trust even the sorters, so detectives had used the secret staircase which was originally there to give access to the clock. Concealing themselves in the roof, they watched through holes in the ceiling the sorting of the mail. Whether in this manner they discovered the thieves I cannot say, but the story was interesting. Now the stairway is blocked up, we invite visitors to tap the wall to see if they can disturb the skeleton.

BANTIE

Father had the front of the coach-house wired in to make a fowl yard. Of all the numerous chooks that lived there, only one found its way to his heart. She was a bantam hen and proved to be a splendid mother. She never missed her broody period and always a setting of eggs were ready to shove under her. Bantie spent a great deal of her time sitting fluffed out over the adopted eggs of her bigger companions. Six eggs were the limit she could manage and she invariably brought out every chick.

Father could never keep his pet Bantie in the fowl yard. In some mysterious way she always seemed to have her freedom. Being small, she managed to squeeze out under the wire-netting that enclosed her home; followed by a brood of chicks almost her size and varying greatly in breed. But that did not worry this good little foster-mother; she treated them all alike and spent a lot of her time scratching up father's garden and watching her chicks trying to imitate her. Father was not amused at her behaviour as she scratched up all his newly planted seedlings. When found, they were scattered in all directions and dried up. For punishment Bantie was placed in a new enclosure, but still she managed to escape.

Father took the entire responsibility of the fowls, keeping their house clean, collecting the eggs and feeding them with waste from the kitchen, plus pollard, bran and seed, mixed in a big tin which made a tasty meal for them. Whilst the mixing was in process Bantie hopped round, hoping that a morsel might be spilt. And if Father turned his back for a moment, Bantie hopped right into the tin and helped herself. When he scolded she made such a fuss and called out so loudly he was forced to give her a special helping to calm her hurt feelings.

Bantie lived a long happy life and when she died she was buried with the accepted ceremony in my pet's cemetery.

YABBY FISHING

We were very fond of yabby fishing, and in the season Father would arrange a picnic. Much preparation was necessary as short sticks had to be cut to which were tied threads of coarse cotton, with pieces of raw meat attached. Marc and I coped with the lines whilst in the kitchen the picnic lunch was prepared.

When the time came for departure and all was ready, off we started in a hired cab. One of these exciting picnics was spent at Marong, a small country town a few miles from Bendigo. We were directed to a pond alleged to be full of yabbies. On arrival we found all to our satisfaction, until the wind blew, and as it came from the direction of the Bone Mills it was most unpleasant. If the wind had not dropped our day would have been spoiled.

After lunch Father, Lorna and I went for a walk. We climbed a hill and were soon in virgin bush country. We gathered wild flowers, whilst Father walked ahead.

When we caught up we found him standing, with his hat in his hand, gazing at a lonely grave. There was a large gum tree growing near, with healed notches in its trunk, and at its base a cairn built of rough stones. There was no inscription to say who lay in that lonely spot. If the tall gum tree that shaded the cairn could only speak it might have told us all. But it was dumb, except for a slight murmur in its leaves.

There is nothing more solemn in a child's life than standing by a grave and thinking of the bodies lying cold beneath the soil. It is so mysterious to realize one must die some day. And so I was glad when Father moved away and Lorna and I were able to run ahead. When we neared the picnic camp we saw a stranger talking to Mother and Aggie. He was the caretaker of the Bone Mills, and had walked over to see if we had caught any yabbies. Father told him of our discovery and asked if he knew the history of the grave. He replied: "It is the burial place of a woman and her two children. A husband, wife and three children had come that way towards Sandhurst, later called Bendigo, in the early Gold Rush days. They had nearly completed their hundred miles journey from Melbourne, when the wife and two of the children took ill with dysentery. It was impossible to get help, so the poor husband and little daughter had to watch them die in the dry bush country. In the hard soil he dug their last resting place, with his own hands, and covering their bodies with bark to act as a coffin, then filled in the grave. The cairn and the notches in the old tree were to mark the spot. After the burial he and his daughter moved on in their lonely caravan to face a life of hardship and strife."

Years later the pioneer's daughter came in search of the grave. She told the caretaker how, in time, her father had prospered and had married again, to bring up a family under very different conditions. When her father died he desired in his Will that the grave be found and cared for.

COCKIE CLAYTON

Our wash house was in a most inconvenient place for the poor woman who came every week to cope with our large wash. Sheets from nine beds, plus numerous other articles, all had to be washed by hand, rinsed and blued and then carried up a steep incline to the top yard in a large basket and hung on the line. Someone had to be called in to help with the load.

In one corner of the large wash house stood a huge cane basket generally full of soiled linen. In this basket we children used to hide under the clothes to get away from Aggie's wrath. When the basket was tipped on its side it made a wonderful playhouse

8

and was generally full of children and pets.

One day when the clothes were all hung on the line, and the poor washerwoman had nearly finished her hard day's work, Cockie Clayton paid us a visit. Cockie was a fine large white cockatoo. He strutted down the backyard and climbed the prop which held the clothes line, now heavy with wet clothes. Dancing a jig, he moved along the line pulling out pegs as he went. And as each sheet dropped on to the dusty ground he threw back his head and roared with laughter. We children could not help joining in the fun, much to the annoyance of the irate washerwoman, who by this time had appeared on the scene. She was so upset at the incident that she immediately gave notice. Mother was cross that we children had taken Cockie's part, and not until he was taken to his home next door and we apologized was the incident forgiven and the washerwoman carried on as usual.

A SEASIDE HOLIDAY

The summer in Bendigo is as hot as the winter is cold, and sometimes weeks and months pass without a drop of rain. The grasses become dry, crisp and brittle, and their seeds cling to everything they touch. The north winds blow the sand from the mines' mullock heaps, causing clouds of dust and forming whirlwinds. After trying days the evenings bring little relief. It was during the hot spell that we were taken to the seaside for a holiday. For many years my parents took a furnished house at Queenscliff overlooking Port Phillip Bay. During one of these holidays I remember seeing my first Movie Picture Show. It was housed in a little oblong tent and was quite a novelty. The operator announced what it was all about and we applauded at the critical moments.

Marc spent most of his time scratching amongst the dry seaweed, or in the scrub looking for dead beetles or other treasures to add to his museum collection, for even then he had started on a naturalist's career. I wanted to help him but he did not always welcome my intrusion. He said I was clumsy and might stand on a delicate crab's back or kick aside a shell of unusual colouring. Seeing I was not wanted, I would go and entertain myself. I had discovered a new game which I played alone; building up reclining figures in the soft damp sand of the seashore. It was a thrilling experience. I gave these effigies seaweed hair, shell eyes and grotesque protruding shell teeth. My efforts were crude and misshaped but they were my first attempts at sculpture. My next efforts were directed to modelling fruit at school. These elementary shapes did not please me, so I broke them up, resoftened the clay with water and modelled it into Grecian Gods and Goddesses. My attempts were amusing, but nevertheless gave me a taste for sculpture which broadened and developed.

Towards the end of our two months holiday we were always happy at the thought of going home for there we would find our pets waiting, the dog to romp with and the cats to cuddle.

BUYING SHEEP

During a drought year Leo bought half-a-dozen sheep at a bargain price. I helped finance the deal. As we had plenty of grass growing in the top yard, Leo thought it would be good fodder for them, but, instead of eating the grass, they escaped to Father's garden. There they had a wonderful time, trampling down treasured shrubs and eating tasty bits from here and there. They played havoc with the vegetable garden. No sooner were they chased back to their enclosure and our backs turned than they would escape again. If the back gate was left open, they would career down the street and out of sight. We were not really sorry until an irate person arrived full of abuse. The sheep were in her garden and refused to be turned out. In despair we sold them to the local butcher for what he would give us.

Leo was full of moneymaking ideas and when Father suggested he cut some wood, he accepted the contract at one shilling a barrow load. After school he brought home a few pals and held a wood chopping competition. He was the referee!

KALOOLA AND BUGGLES

Marc owned a horse called "Kaloola." When his interest in riding flagged, he sold her to Leo who was rapidly developing into a handsome youth. Mounted on "Kaloola" in his new riding outfit he looked fine.

One morning he rode into the factory yard whilst Father was interviewing a commercial traveller who was trying to sell him some goods. Father interrupted the business to remark: "That is my son on horseback," but the traveller took no notice and continued to quote prices, obviously too intent on an order to notice the fine specimen of manhood on horseback. Needless to say, he went away minus an order.

Early in the year 1914 Leo had to sell "Kaloola" because food was expensive owing to the drought. The parting was difficult as he had become attached to the horse, and, not expecting to see him again, patted him "Goodbye." But that was not the end of the story. On Leo's 18th birthday he enlisted in the Eighth Light Horse

Brigade. When he entered camp in 1915 "Kaloola" was there to greet him. Having recognized his voice, she neighed a welcome. She too was a hero of that Bloody War.

Buggles, our fluffy silver headed little dog, was a great favourite with we children, but not with Father, who complained because he would bark at the slightest noise and run up and down the lawn, wearing a track and yapping at all who passed. Nothing we could do would break him of the habit, and at last it became so bad that Father insisted he be given away. For many months we heard little of Buggles but were told he had a good home.

The day Leo came home to tell us that he had enlisted and been accepted for the army we three girls thought him a hero and immediately discussed what we could knit for his comfort. But the news went deeper with Mother and Father. They were sad and silent. At this critical moment, a dirty, crestfallen little urchin of a dog crept into the sitting room. On seeing him our excitement was intense and outshone any depression we were feeling and the only tears we shed were the tears of joy. We smothered our little pet with affection. Then Leo spoke up and said, "Dad you simply must let us keep him, if only as a mascot" - and of course he did.

TOOIE

As a school boy Leo exchanged two pigeons for a pink and grey galah. He called her Tooie. She was very faithful and gave all her love to him. Each morning she would find her way to his room, climb up the bedclothes and nestle in the curve of his arm and if anyone came near she would become pugnacious and show fight. While Leo was at school Tooie would amuse herself by scraping holes in the plaster wall above the doors. At four o'clock she regularly went to the front of the house, perched on the rail of the verandah and there waited until she heard Leo coming home. At the first sound of his voice she screeched a welcome.

Tooie also acted as a mascot and lived through the four years Leo was away. The day we got a cable saying "Kill the fatted calf am sailing for home", poor little Tooie died.

I DECIDED ON MY CAREER

When I was twelve years old, and Lorna a little older, we went to the Bendigo School of Mines on Saturday to learn drawing. After the class we would creep into the modelling room to watch students at work. One of them, to our tender years, appeared very old. He wore a nightshirt in place of an overall and so we named him "Old Nightshirt." One day he took my small hand in his broad palm and said to his companions "Look at this child's hand, it is the hand of a sculptor." This remark impressed me and from that moment I was seething with ambition and had decided on my career. After studying in Bendigo and in Melbourne, I was sent abroad to continue my studies at the Royal College of Art, London. During the five years I was there I had to live without a pet of any sort. For consolation I spent a lot of time at the Zoo. Asking for a student's pass from the college, I would set off for the day with a sketch book and some lunch in a haversack slung over my shoulder. I would spend the day sketching the creatures I wanted to use in my work. I had designed a fountain in the Architectural School and was busy building it into a sketch model. In the centre I had placed a sea lion with his head tilted heaven-wards, so that his mouth could spout water. Round the outer rim of the pond I placed four penguins quietly sunning themselves. I was not well acquainted with these creatures, so went to the Zoo intent on drawing some. I found my ambition much above my ability for none of them would stay still for one moment. In despair I put my book away and for hours stood mentally studying the slightest functioning of their supple bodies. I watched the fat old sea lion sway his head from side to side as he bellowed for his tea. And the little squat penguin, with his shiny white breast and clumsy feet. I made a number of mental notes of their habits before returning to continue my work at College. Whilst the memory was still fresh, I lost no time in building up a model of the fat old sea lion that dominated the pool, and the smug little penguins pruning their oily feathers.

I have visited many Zoos; Edinburgh, Dublin, Ceylon, Paris, Antwerp, Munich, Hamburg, Berlin, and many others, and not one of them could take the place that the London Zoo held in my heart. I casually mentioned this to some student friends and said that I would dearly like to take some poor children to the Zoo. We secured ten slum kiddies from the Police Mission and gave them wonderful time. They were a little frightened of us at first, but soon gained confidence, the joy of feeding the monkey and the bears, and watching the seals having their afternoon meal and the pleasure of a ride on the elephant's back soon made them forget their self-consciousness. As one interest after another presented itself, the children's excitement grew beyond all bounds. They were much too busy to think of eating and gave most of their lunch away to the poor beasts behind their prison bars. We had brought a great deal of food, thinking the kiddies would need nourishment, but food did not interest them, only the pleasure of giving it away, and the outing.

ST. IVES.

"As I was going to St. Ives I met a man with seven wives," at least I concluded he must have that many. And that "each wife had seven cats and each cat had seven kits," for there were cats every-where. I am sure nothing had changed in this quaint old-world fishing village since the days the nursery rhyme was written.

There were cats on the walls, in doorways, and sunning themselves in the middle of the road and running up to meet you as you passed, to rub against your leg and look up into your face with big staring bright eyes as if to say "Welcome to our village, we will show you round and keep you entertained." And so they did, I walked ahead, and from every corner new cats appeared and followed me. If I had had a flute I could have led them "Over the hill and far away."

Most people I met on my wandering through the village and by-ways, looked as old and worn as the buildings they frequented. The roads were packed close together, admitting very little sunshine and air. I saw no new buildings; and no new buildings would fit into the St. Ives' environment.

Walking for many hours over the hard cobble stone roads, admiring the small homes huddled close together, I wondered whether these houses possessed any backyards as clothes were hung out on lines in the front.

The village is so attractive and paintable that many of the fishermen's cottages had been turned into artists' studios. I visited one that was open to the public. An exhibition was on view, it was housed in a sort of loft, which was only accessible by climbing steep stone steps without any railing for support.

After absorbing as much of the village as possible in the short time I had, I made for the beach to sit on the sand and rest. In the middle of the little harbour I watched ships come home, bringing loads of fish for market. There were hundreds of species similar to our Australian gummy shark. These fish were skinned and gutted on the beach and the innards thrown to the seagulls, who fought and chased each other whilst devouring these unsightly entrails. When gutted and washed in fresh seawater, the fish were packed and sent straight to London to be sold as rock salmon.

I watched with interest each step of the procedure and whilst I squatted on the sand was joined by village children. When I told them I had come from far off Australia their eyes opened wide with wonder and many strange and quaint questions were asked, all of which I answered as best I could. Then taking them to the village I

13

bought them sweets. They did not leave until it was time for me to go, then they followed to the bus and waved "Goodbye." As I journeyed further away I thought of those poorly clad unspoilt children of the fisher folk of St. Ives and I enjoyed my thoughts.

DREAMING DREAMS

The English forests are so different from our Bushland and to visit them in Autumn is a great treat to watch the lovely trees shaking their golden leaves to the ground and carpeting the earth with their soft brown shades. I love to walk on the fallen leaves and sometimes, squatting Buddha like, sink into their discarded foliage and there meditate and dream of fairy folk. And dreaming dreams, I see these little people. They smile at me then fade as quickly as they came.

Still squatting in my primitive bed, I heard movement in some dry crisp leaves, and turning my head I saw a little squirrel close at hand. He sat upright and in his paws held an acorn. Nibbling away the outer crust he started to eat the sweet kernel. I watched him through his meal and saw him go in search of more, and, although conscious of my presence, he did not seem to mind the intrusion. I think he rather appreciated company.

As the sun was dipping towards the horizon, I knew it was time to stir my lazy bones and leave this enchanted wood and wander my way home. Such days as these are not easily forgotten and often the falling of a golden leaf will bring back memories of student days and of days spent in the heart of an English forest.

AN ISLAND FULL OF INTEREST

Arriving back in Australia after five years abroad, and having had the privilege of being able to study under the inspired influence of Henry Moore, I found it difficult to settle down to the work of establishing myself as a sculptor. I was still impregnated with the wanderlust and for the first few years took extensive holidays, visiting interstate and New Zealand. But the holidays I really enjoy are those spent at Cowes on Phillip Island. The Island is declared a sanctuary for the strange and unusual creatures that make it their home. Phillip Island is so crammed full of history that not a day of my holiday passes without me hearing something of new interest. The personalities past and present are living souls to me and so I feel I must depart from the main thread of my story to tell you a few asides.

SEALS

On the rocks called "The Nobbies," which raise their shaggy heads above the water a mile off the south-west corner of the Island, live thousands of seals. There they reign supreme, protected by their bull who mounts guard over his extensive harem, whilst his ladies lie in perfect comfort, curled up nose to tail. When disturbed they flip-flop across the rugged face of the rocks and like giant slugs plunge into the angry sea. There they frolic and play a hide-and-seek game, and roar the while, making a hideous noise, as if to frighten away curious on-lookers who in a pleasure boat spy on them and idle away time in holiday spirit.

PENGUINS

Facing the ocean, between great rocky cliffs and jutting headlands, sand dunes run up sharply from the beach for about two or three hundred feet, merging into undulating plains. These are overgrown with coarse reedy grass which holds the sand in place, and keeps it from shifting off its wind-blown surface. In these beds of waving grass the small fairy penguins dig their burrows. They are strange birds of ancient origin who live mostly under the water. Having lost the quills in their feathers, they overlap like scales and cover their bodies with a soft glossy down. The wings are useless for flight and have grown thin and evolved into paddles, which are used in a similar manner as the fins of a fish. In late September or early in October they come ashore for the mating season, find their old burrows and clean them out, or, if newlywed, dig a new one; and for the next few months these little creatures are busy with domestic duties. After laying two eggs the female stands upright over them, thus making a dent in the base of her body, which covers the eggs and keeps them warm until the chicks emerge. The male, in true fatherly fashion, hunts in the depth of the sea to supply food during the incubating period, later, when the chicks are fully fledged, his mate joins him in the arduous effort of supplying sustenance.

At the end of each day, when the light has faded, these little bread-winners meet at the water's edge, and when all have assembled they march in formation over the sand and struggle up the steep cliff leading to their burrows. Their pouches are loaded with fish for the hungry chicks awaiting their return.

These unique penguins are not allowed any more privacy than the majestic seals, for sightseers with their strong torches lie in wait for them to spy and upset their general routine by suddenly flashing gleaming lights in their eyes. The sudden brightness frightens the little birds into disorder, making some scurry back towards the water, whilst others scatter over the sand in all directions. Some are only delayed in their home-coming, but others are so scared that they vomit the fish that has taken them all day to collect for their youngsters who are waiting at the entrance of their burrows, all eager for the promised feed. If the feed is not forthcoming, then the poor chicks have to go hungry for another twenty-four hours. However, this wanton selfishness on the part of onlookers is no longer tolerated. The parade ground of these diligent birds is now walled off and artificially lit, and guides are there to control the crowds. I was glad to see this improvement on some of my recent visits, for already I have spent eighteen holidays in Cowes.

MUTTON BIRDS

From about the 21st to the 26th of November each year the mutton birds arrive in flocks, emigrating from foreign regions. For a while the sky is darkened by their number and the sight of these sooty coloured, large-wing-spanned creatures of the air is astonishing. Each year the older birds return to the same burrow, whilst the younger and newly-mated scrape, with their strong talons, a new home. The burrow that encloses the nest is dug a few feet into the ground, much as a rabbit's home. It is generally built under the protection of a clump of wind-blown reeds which lean earthward over the entrance, as if to shield the bird from the inquisitive eye of man. For someone is always ready in idle curiosity to interfere, or else in a selfish desire to rob the nest of its eggs. These are considered good to eat, as is the bird itself, although the latter is rich in oil and not palatable to the finer taste.

The mutton birds, the penguins, and the rabbits all turn the southern and western corners of the Island into traps for the unwary feet. For they undermine the ground in all directions and one has to be careful where one treads, for underneath may be a mutton bird baby, a small family of bunnies, or a pair of penguin chicks. Besides, in the latter part of the season, the adult penguin moults and through this period of about two weeks it lives in its burrow on its own fat and until fully plumed with new season's feathers. During this time it loses so much weight that it has to swallow stones in order to submerge when taking to the sea again.

ABORIGINAL KITCHENS

Here and there throughout the island are remains of antique Aboriginal kitchens. These consist of piles of shells, some scattered thickly on the ground and some embedded in the broken sides of sand dunes, where once the Aboriginal man feasted on shellfish undisturbed.

Many of these camping grounds I discovered in remote parts of the island and, sitting on the ground close at hand, my mind carried me back in time when the Aboriginal owned this fair island and lived there in a paradise of plenty.

SKIPPER COX

As late as 1920 there lived an old identity of the island called Skipper Cox. He was then about eighty years of age. In his early life he had a cottage where the National Bank now stands. When his wife died he no longer wished for civilized life, so retired to the seashore and there built himself a hut out of driftwood, shaped round the hollow of a curved rocky background. This helped to shelter the shipshape structure. He added a most unusual workhouse, the roof of which comprised an old wrecked boat turned upside down which had been washed ashore and had conveniently landed in his seaweed garden. Propped about five feet from the ground with the aid of driftwood, it was just high enough to admit him. He was a frail little man with untidy grey hair, a short beard, sharp features and sparkling blue eyes which shone with good nature and foretold a keen sense of humour. Although apparently so frail this little man must have possessed great strength, for on certain days of the week he sailed a boat over many miles to Sandy Point. There he delivered passengers, the mail and freshly caught fish into the hands of a driver of a Cobb & Co's coach which was waiting on the shore. In stormy weather the journey must have been perilous, for his boat was so heavily laden that it was scarcely out of the water.

In his workshop he extracted oil from sharks and stingrays caught from the side of his much used boat. This he bottled as an embrocation and ointment and claimed it would cure all sorts of ailments.

Stepping from his boat after a day's fishing excursion he was met by many cats, who mysteriously appeared from all directions. They followed him home as if he was the Pied Piper. One large ginger Tom seemed to be his favourite and when feeding the cats on freshly caught fish, Tom always got more than his share. Perhaps because he rubbed more than the others against the old man's leg, or was it because he liked to curl up on the skipper's lap when he sat in the sun smoking his stale old clay pipe?

From his doorway he sold fish and choice shells, for in those days there was no old age pension.

Visitors were always welcome to his home and if a shy young female made an appearance he would rise and say "God bless you, my dear, my heart is so full, I cannot kiss you."

The beach has changed, the hut has disappeared, but the skipper's memory is still fresh in many minds. He disappeared mysteriously one stormy night, when the wind was howling and the waves were destroying all within their reach. What happened no one knows. Some suspected foul play, as a suspicious character, who was round the village at the time, also disappeared. But we will hope that the gods were kind to this much loved sailor and blew his frail body out to sea, so that his spirit could wander in a phantom ship over the waves from shore to shore.

ELIZA COGHLAN

Another character of the island was Eliza Coghlan. She lived to the great age of one hundred and thirteen years. A native of Ireland she was naturally at home on a farm and slaved at her work from dawn to dark. This old woman, without a tooth in her head, must have had a strong body, for even when she reached her century she still trudged five miles to Cowes carrying a live turkey under each arm to sell to the local hotel. When she had delivered her heavy load, she would start on her return journey.

"BROADWATER"

My first holiday at Cowes was spent at a popular Guest House full of noisy people. I was not happy in their company, so would wander alone to enjoy solitude and to get as far as possible from holiday-makers. On these pleasant walks I would seek the Koala, who is to be found curled up in the forks of the gum trees. These lazy little fellows are generally asleep in the daytime, but with a little persuasion will open an eye to see who rudely disturbs their slumbers. If within reach, they will disdainfully take a branch picked from a sweet Manna Gum tree and in a half dreamy fashion nibble the choicest leaves.

These strange little creatures have no tails and, as usual with marsupials, the female has a pouch in which to carry her young. As soon as the baby is old enough to crawl, it either clings to its mother's back, or curls up and goes to sleep in her arms. In true motherly fashion she holds it close and feeds it on sweet milk from her breasts.

I am never tired of looking at these bushy soft looking balls of fur, and always the desire creeps into my mind to have one as a pet. But that would never do for the island is a reserve for these creatures who are under the protection of the government, and so can live unmolested. They sleep away the day, and at night move round to enjoy the freedom of their island home. These small Koala were originally brought from the mainland by the early settlers, but the wallaby seems to be a native and is still to be found in the wilder parts of the island.

THE BUILDING OF "BROADWATER"

As many of the inhabitants are descendants of pioneers, they have much to tell. Whilst the local baker filled his oven with uncooked bread he told me how he had watched timber and other building materials being unloaded from a boat and dumped on the shore when he was a young boy. Week by week, and month by month he saw the building of "Broadwater", the home of Mrs. Henty Wilson, a daughter of one of the Henty Brothers who founded the first permanent white settlement in Victoria. The old home is now a Guest House, having belonged to Mr. & Mrs. Oswin-Roberts. It nestles in flat country amongst tall Banksia trees and bending Ti-trees and is only a stone's throw from the seashore. After discovering the place I have never wanted to stay anywhere else, and every year or so I make my way to "Broadwater", and there live in a bungalow away from the main house.

MEETING THE OSWIN-ROBERTS

When Mr. & Mrs. Roberts were alive they had special permission from the Chief Inspector of Fisheries and Game to care for maimed or abandoned baby Koalas whose mothers had been killed through some mishap.

I shall never forget the first day I met Mrs. Roberts. I had sunk into the soft cushions of a comfortable armchair and was entertaining myself gazing at a shelf that ran round the upper part of the walls of the lounge room of "Broadwater". On this shelf were placed many and varied images of birds cleverly made from cones of the Banksia tree by Mr. Roberts. They were all shapes and poses, some tall and slender, whilst others were short and broad. Each expressed a mood, and were so human in appearance that they reminded me of many friends and acquaintances.

Soon the door at the far end of the room opened and Mrs. Roberts appeared, a tall dignified lady with a stately tread. On her shoulder sat a three-months old Koala. Her husband followed her carrying a heavier Koala. They passed through the lounge into a large dance or play-room. I joined a large audience that had gathered to see the sleepy Koalas drink warm milk from a silver spoon, or nibble away at a rosy ripe apple. Then a third Koala was brought in and the same performance repeated.

Showing signs of satisfaction and sleepiness, the three Koalas were carried away and the visitors left after buying a shilling button. The money went towards a fund to buy Manna Gum trees to plant a forest for future Koalas.

I never tired of seeing the Roberts' pets and stroking upwards their fur, for they do not like you to stroke the usual way, and are quite likely to get angry if you did.

"PIX" REPRESENTATIVE TAKES PHOTOGRAPHS

I was sorry when my holiday came to an end, and I had to leave Cowes, for I was impressed with the place and resolved to go there again. The opportunity came quicker than I expected. A photographer who represented "Pix", an illustrated magazine, called with the idea of taking a series of photographs of me, my studio, my work and my home for his paper. Whilst he prepared his camera I told of the Koalas I had seen at "Broadwater", of their almost human behaviour and of the ardent love they possessed for their foster-parents. He was immediately impressed and considered taking a series of photographs for "Pix". A weekend was arranged and I was asked to join the party.

When the eventful time came, we set off in two cars for Stony Point and crossed by ferry. It was very cold and we were glad on arrival to find a hot dinner waiting and also a happy welcome.

Later in the afternoon the party was introduced to each Koala in turn. Edwin was the first. He was found snugly tucked away under a water tank, in a shelter built of Ti-tree sticks bound closely together. It was a neat little home with the dead limb of a tree placed for him to climb with plenty of succulent gum leaves within reach. Sitting curled up in a fork of this limb he snoozed oblivious of the intrusion, so not caring to interfere with his slumber we crept quietly away.

The next to be introduced was the baby, who was in even more cosy surroundings, for he was asleep in a clothes basket in his foster-parents' bedroom. With the opening of the lid the little creature awoke, yawned, rubbed his eyes, and seeing that we looked friendly souls, climbed out of bed and into the arms of Mrs. Roberts. She carried him into the office and we all sat down for a yarn and a cup of tea. By this time the baby was fully awake, and after drinking a few spoonsful of milk, thought it was time to show off. So climbing onto his mistress' shoulder, then her head, he grabbed the curtain and with nimble limbs climbed to the pole. There leaning against the wall in a half drunken fashion went to sleep. And so we left him and went in search of Edward, whom we found lying full length on his back in a hammock hung between two trees, with a colourful umbrella arranged above to keep off the weather.

Seeing his mistress approaching, Edward made no pretence to hide his emotional feelings and without hesitation climbed into her arms, for no ordinary love linked them. She had reared and tended the little Koala since babyhood. Children who were staying at "Broadwater" had found him in the fork of a tree. No mother was about and, although they searched until nightfall, she did not appear. The children covered the little Koala with a woolly shawl to keep it warm and prayed that it would come to no harm. In the morning the little stray was no longer in the tree but cuddled in the arms of Mrs. Roberts. This great spiritual mother of the Koalas had given it a home.

Under her care Edward thrived and from a thin little fellow grew to a bouncing baby. When old enough the little Koala was christened at a formal dinner party given to celebrate the adoption. The guest of honour was Mr. Frederick Lewis, Chief Inspector of Fisheries & Game. The wee thing was christened "Edward Lewis Oswin-Roberts, Esq." During the ceremony the little creature sat upright in a baby's high chair, drank warm sweetened milk, nibbled choice Manna Gum leaves, and thoroughly enjoyed the party. I listened to the story of this ceremony and entertainment as it was recounted to "Pix" representative.

IT WAS TOO LATE TO CHANGE HER NAME

Not until later was it discovered that Edward had a pouch, then it was too late to change her name. In hot weather she lay back in a chair, and, with a blissful air, posed whilst her mistress fanned her with a fan which once belonged to Queen Victoria. All this spoiling she took with ease, and at night she slept on cushions in a comfortable arm chair at the foot of her foster parents' bed. In the morning she climbed to the floor, (for at this time she was no larger than a kitten), and walking across to the bed would ask in Koala language to be picked up. In a half dreamy fashion Mrs. Roberts would put a hand out and little Edward would place her paw in it, and so be raised from the ground and drawn under the warm blankets to sleep out the rest of the early morning. When older she was placed in a large gum tree opposite the gateway so that she could have her freedom, but not caring for it was glad to come down at night and be put to bed in her usual place.

The old gum tree still thrives and lives on as a memorial to Edward. It bears a bronze plate recording the famous little Koala's history.

ONE DAY EDWARD DISAPPEARED

One day Edward disappeared and Mrs. Robert's heart was wrung with grief. They searched everywhere but could not find her. When they had abandoned all hope they discovered the wee thing in the pantry, tucked inside a brown paper bag and nibbling away at a bunch of grapes. It was thought the Koalas would eat nothing but gum leaves and anxiety was felt in case the strange meal killed her. But as days passed she grew stronger instead of weaker and often indulged in a meal of ripe plums or sweet juicy apples.

When the Roberts went for a holiday they took Edward with them. She loved these excursions and would lounge back in the car as if she was its owner, or climb onto her foster mother's knees and watch from the window. These were happy days for these three were never parted and to consider a separation was out of the question.

When asked by a friend why they did not take a trip to England, Mrs. Roberts replied: "How could we possibly go to England and leave Edward?" And of course they did not go to England, nor did they leave Edward during the seven years she lived in their care.

They had special permission from the Chief Inspector of Fisheries and Game to rear the little Koala, and they did their duty nobly, not only towards Edward, but to all injured or neglected Koalas who were brought to "Broadwater" to be cared for. When strong and well again they were given their freedom and placed in a bushy gum tree and allowed to wander at will.

There was no other creature in Australia better known than Edward during her life, for she was written up so often and received so many visitors that her fame spread to other countries, and when she died there were many mourners. But no one mourned as her foster mother, for her darling pet had gone and no other pet could take her place. No longer would one see Mrs. Roberts sitting by the fire, rocking Edward to sleep, talking to her in Koala language she could understand, the little Koala answering in soft, sweet little grunts, as if to say "Yes! I am very happy." Then a look of contentment would pass over their faces and Edward would seem to smile, then close her eyes in sleep.

When it was known that Edward was ailing the greatest attention was given to her, but nothing could save her life. Her little body was brought to Melbourne for a post-mortem, her fur sent to a taxidermist, so that she could be preserved as a museum piece, and her remains were buried in the garden of the late Mr. Ambrose Pratt, at Surrey Hills, Victoria,

BEFORE RECEIVING OFFICIAL PERMISSION

Before Mrs. Roberts received official permission to care for injured Koalas she had a dramatic experience with a Koala she called "Orace." He, poor baby thing, was found at the foot of a tree with a broken forearm. When placed on a branch it was found he could not climb. If it had been neglected he would only have starved, so Mrs. Roberts took him indoors, bound his injured arm and nursed him carefully. All was going well when, unexpectedly, the police interfered. They demanded "Orace's" release immediately, but Mrs. Roberts would not hear of such nonsense, she would rather have gone to gaol than release him, for in his poor state of health he would surely have died, or have been killed by dogs.

The morning after the police interference Mr. Roberts rang the Chief Inspector of Fisheries and Game and explained the case, and of course was given permission to nurse "Orace" back to health before releasing him.

NESTING IN THE BOWL OF A TREE FERN

No stray dog was chased away from "Broadwater", although not encouraged to stay, for dogs have a habit of getting into mischief. Cats breed oblivious to restraint and live undisturbed under cover of the bungalow floors; and in the thick foliage of trees, birds of both day and night call their notes.

In these trees many birds are to be seen. Once one was discovered nesting in the bowl of a Fern Tree. As the fronds opened the nest rose with their growth and came further into view, exposing the chicks to the sun, wind and rain. Thinking the babies would suffer in their nudity, Mrs. Roberts, in her usual big-hearted way, had a colourful umbrella placed above the nest, so that when the sun shone, or it poured with rain, the birdies would be quite comfortable and happy.

PERCY

Percy does the odd jobs about "Broadwater". He is not much over four feet in height. Although so small, he is perfectly proportioned and has a handsome, agreeable face. Percy has been at "Broadwater" for nearly fifty years and now considers it his home. If ever told to leave, he takes no notice and stays from year to year. During my many visits I often came across him wheeling round narrow winding paths a huge barrow, full of refuse for the fowls, and followed by a dozen or more cats. Frequent visitors are so accustomed to him that he seems to them as part of the tradition of the old home. And children follow Percy as if he was one of them. He leads like the Pied Piper, but he does not play a flute, only smiles and speaks a language that children understand.

BUSH FIRES

In an obituary notice which appeared in the "Galloway Gazette" of the 21st March, 1903, it stated that, "On his first arrival on the island Mr. McHaffie cleared it by setting fire to the scrub, and the reflection from the fire that enveloped the whole island attracted attention for several days and nights in the adjacent continent and far out to sea."

That was the first fire recorded on Phillip Island. There have been others since, one of the worst in February 1944. This was a disastrous affair. Starting about a mile from "Broadwater", it blazed with great ferocity and in four minutes swept through the whole sanctuary. The forest that had been protected was burnt as black as cinders.

Some Koalas made their way to the sea and drank salt water, a thing unheard of as these little creatures are supposed not to drink in their natural state. On the ground and in forks of trees were found dead, dying, and injured Koalas. All who could be saved were brought to "Broadwater" and two large bungalows were turned into hospital wards to house these poor little Koalas. Net hammocks were made and hung across the room and in each of these four patients were laid. Nurses and helpers from animal institutions came to the fore and also guests staying at "Broadwater" made themselves as useful as they could. Every night sixty-eight dressings had to be changed and the sick Koalas had to be hand-fed. As the doors of the bungalows opened each morning all the patients' little heads popped up as if to say, "Hurry up, we are waiting for you to come". When they were all well enough they were laid on rugs on the tennis court to get a sunning, and with whisks of Ti-tree the flies were fanned away. As their health returned they began to quarrel amongst themselves. This was a good sign, for soon they would be able to be released in the part of the forest untouched by ravenous fire.

A great many of the trees were burnt, and as there was not sufficient food left on the island, fourteen hundred Koalas had to be taken to the mainland.

Since a more recent fire, more have been taken and placed in suitable forests. There are still a great number of Koalas on the island, but now they seem to be well provided for as Mrs. Roberts left by her will a bequest that two hundred acres of forest land be set aside as an extra sanctuary for her much loved Koalas.

THE FAIRIES' TREE

Although I suffered with the wander lust after my return from England, I still had time to work and concentrated on the powers that lie behind all inspiration, I became very happy and with my thoughts centred on my work. Life grew so full that scarcely a minute was wasted. From early morning until late at night I stuck to my job. Slogging away at some sculptural conception, or doing something almost as strenuous, my body became strong and powerful under the strain. I began to take on the bearing of a sculptor, people accepted me as such, and then life became very interesting. Not only was I gaining knowledge of my work, but also a philosophy. I was rubbing shoulders with humanity, I belonged to them and all personal feeling had to be controlled, as I had schooled myself to become one with all types of people. However much I wanted to rest in seclusion, I could not do so, my body and soul were not my own. I had dedicated them to my work. Otherwise, I could not have taken on the arduous job of carving the "Fairies' Tree" for although it was a labour of love, it demanded hard and strenuous effort.

This is how it first came about. Towards the end of my five years' study at the Royal College of Art, London, I saw the "Elfin Oak" in Kensington Gardens. I was led to it by two fellow students. They had discovered it by accident a few days before, and were so excited by its charm and beauty, they talked of nothing else, and were not content until they had taken me to see it.

Time, mist, and cold were forgotten as we walked round that wonderful dead old tree which was carved into a fairyland for children.

"How I would like to carve a tree like the "Elfin Oak" for the children of Australia", I exclaimed.

25

With that utterance the seed of my "Fairies' Tree" was born. The more I contemplated the idea, the more the seed swelled, and by the time I arrived back in Australia, on the 4th of December, 1930, I had built such a magnificent conception that my tree already lived in my imagination. The only thing that remained was for me to materialize the idea as quickly as possible. First I had to find a tree in a suitable place and to get official permission to carve it. One day a friend called, and knowing he was familiar with every tree of importance in Melbourne, I immediately asked his help. Without hesitation he led me to the Fitzroy Gardens. There he showed me an old knotted Blue Gum trunk.

"Is this what you want?" he asked.

"Yes!" I replied, "it is just made for the Little People. Round this old tree I will build up fairy lore. I will create a place of peace, a place that will make everyone happy, however sad and weary they may be at heart."

I did not know then of all the unhappiness and humiliation I would have to suffer in order to create a happy place. But it is all over now and, as the years go by, the love I put into that tree will grow bigger and bigger and expand into other corners of the earth.

I RENT A STUDIO

On the 5th of January, 1931, only a few weeks after I arrived back in Australia after my five years' study abroad, I rented a studio at No. 9 Collins Street, Melbourne. The pieces of sculpture I had produced whilst I was a student in London had been stored at the Customs House. When brought to No. 9 they were unpacked in the presence of a Customs Official and I was made to pay duty on my own productions.

After placing my work around the walls of my studio, I proceeded to produce more as in March of that year I was to have an exhibition and there was no time to be lost.

The radio station 3.D.B. had invited me to give a talk on sculpture. I was nervous of voicing my opinion, and had always avoided doing so, but as my exhibition was to be held almost immediately and I wanted the publicity I decided to show courage and accepted the invitation. In due course I gave my talk. It seemed to please, as it was suggested that I give another about the tree I told them I hoped to carve. As I had not yet been given permission to carry out my scheme, I decided I had better seek

The Fairies' Tree

27

Detail of Tree

it as soon as possible. The first step led me to the Town Hall and then to interview Dr. Kent Hughes, Chairman of the Parks & Gardens Committee. He happened to be a man with a vivid imagination and was so delighted with the idea that he came with me straight away to see the tree I wanted to carve. There were two in the Fitzroy Gardens that were possible, but since one had had the bark cut away to make an Aboriginal canoe I would not touch it, thinking it sacred to the Aboriginal people. The other was as if made for the purpose.

I COMMENCE TO CARVE

Early in May, 1931, I collected my tools and mallet, donned my blue smocked overall and walked across the gardens to start on my three years work, which ended precisely in May, 1934. I did not realize what a tremendous task I had undertaken, otherwise I would not have had the heart to begin.

THE FIRE

The old tree's trunk was covered with lumps and blisters, caused when it caught fire many years ago. The theory put forward to explain this was that a magpie, who was known to have a nest in the tree, had carried a lighted cigarette into the hollow of its trunk. Soon the tree's heart was on fire, with smoke belching forth from the interior, giving the effect of a great chimney-stack ablaze. The glow lit up the sky and many people, attracted by the glare, ran to see what was the matter. When the Fire Brigade arrived the firemen had to push their way through the dense crowd before they could take control and quench the flame. They were too late to save the tree, for its heart had stopped beating and only the trunk had been left.

The husk of the old tree, with hundreds of years to its credit, still stands as a memento of the Aboriginals, who once danced their corroborees in its shade. At its base ivy had grown, caressing its worn form as if to protect it for all times. Bees had built their home in the heart of the dead tree, turning it into a palace of gold for the fairies to enjoy.

BEES WERE NOT MY ONLY ANNOYANCE

When my mallet struck the tree the bees showed their objection by attacking me, one stinging me on the eyelid for my impertinence. I realized I must have deserved this treatment, having driven my chisel rather deeply into the knarled trunk on a hollow spot just below the great tree's dead heart. To them it was sacred. Soon my eye swelled alarmingly. From the garden kiosk I borrowed a blue-bag and dabbed it on the already swollen eye, giving me a theatrical appearance, then, turning my back on my usual audience who collected to watch me work, I continued, much to the bees' displeasure.

The mosquitoes were my next annoyance, as well as a very small insect which disguised itself by carrying dirt on its back. When working I was continuously stung on the foot, and looking at my instep, would brush what appeared to be a piece of dirt from it. These stinging bits of matter continued to worry and aggravate me for some time, until I became suspicious and examined them closely. I found them not bits of dirt but small insects disguised as such. But these small mites were trivial when compared with humans. They distracted me by trying to draw me into conversation and by asking silly questions. One woman wanted to know how old the tree was, and when I told her about five or six hundred years she contradicted me by saying, "It could not be as Melbourne was only a hundred years old."

An amusing remark was made by two urchins who were passing by. One said, "Who done this?" The other replied, "Nobody done it, only a lady." And so they passed on with no more than a glance in my direction. The next offender was a carpenter. "Why did I not plane off all the notches and have a smooth surface on which to work?" he asked. The notches are my fairies and creatures and my problem was how little I should carve away, in order not to lose the natural shape, keeping them far from the naturalistic and as much part of the tree as possible. I wanted to create a mystery and make the carvings to appear as part of the natural growth.

One day a loud and talkative woman, who was not very sober, insisted that I was carving Demi-Gods on the tree. She was quite annoyed when I laughed, unaware of her seriousness. Then a man asked "Are you the tart who carved the tree?" And when I replied "Yes", he wrung my hand. But my worries were not all amusing as some people were abusive and quite vicious and even damaged the carvings by cutting bits out of them with a penknife, whilst others carved their names on the tree. But despite this vandalism, I worked on, sometimes squatting on the ground in a doubled-up position, sometimes on the top rung of a very insecure ladder. Seldom was I able to work in a comfortable position, but I laboured on despite inconveniences.

As the carvings progressed they caused much interest and for their protection an iron railing was placed round the tree. Before this was done a tortoise and a snail had been wrenched from the tree, so the precautions were justified.

POISONED WHEAT

Most nights I worked on the tree until the light failed, then trudged home to my lonely studio. One evening I was pleased to find a fellow sculptor waiting for me. We were colleagues who had studied most of our student years at the same schools of art. He had his arms full of food brought to share with me.

After dining well in the open space of the studio, we disappeared down the few steps to the vault-like kitchen to wash the dishes, On a shelf near the stove I had placed a saucer of poisoned wheat. Whilst flourishing the cloth in an endeavour to dry the dishes thoroughly, my fellow-sculptor chewed wheat from the saucer. Being busy washing up I did not notice my guest was still hungry and that he was nibbling away at the mouse trap bait. Suddenly I discovered what he was doing and staring at him with fear in my eyes, I exclaimed "Are you trying to commit suicide? You are eating poisoned wheat!" Making a dash for the sink he coughed and spluttered in an endeavour to dislodge the devoured grains, but it was of no avail.

Later, when I bid my rival "Goodbye," with tears in my eyes and a lump in my throat, I thought perhaps I would never see him again. But I was mistaken for the next day he blew along all smiles and looking the picture of health. Now I know how it is that mice thrive on poisoned wheat.

BECOMING A SCHOOL "MARM"

In 1933 I relieved the Art Mistress of the Geelong Church of England Boys' Grammar School, whilst she took a five months' trip abroad. I was nervous of the post as I had none of the learned or academic qualities that suited the position. I was simply a natural artist, feeling, thinking and acting on inspiration. And I had not the slightest idea how to manage schoolboys, but I soon learnt, not only to manage them, but to become their friend. And some of those small boys, now grown to big men, are still my pals.

Before I stepped into this new experience, I had only visited the school on one occasion. An interview had been arranged for discussion regarding the designing of a memorial panel for the library, to be carved in blackwood. Whilst on this visit I had a good opportunity to view the school and its surroundings and splendid layout. Situated a few miles from Geelong, it nestles on the edge of Corio Bay. Most of the buildings are of the Gothic style and give the impression of a Mediaeval self-contained city. The whole effect and atmosphere is most pleasing, and so when later I was invited to become a member of the staff for a short time, I accepted with pleasure, though with diffidence.

When I arrived to take up duty I was given a small flat to occupy whilst in residence. It was across the road from the main buildings and it consisted of a bedroom, a sitting-room and a bath-room. My sole companion was Black Friar, a small half-grown kitten who was placed in my charge by its former owner. As time went on I became very fond of this small black creature who was always about to greet me when I left the class-room. I was glad of the cat's company as I was very lonely, for all the other teachers were male and had wives to keep them company.

When off duty I spent most of my time walking. Beginning at one end of the school ground and walking the complete bend of the seashore, I would end up at the boundary of the grounds. Then back I would go across the fields to my lonely room where there were no tools or clay to dabble with and nothing to do but read or write in an unsympathetic atmosphere, or stroke the cat who had crawled onto my lap. In this way Black Friar and I became inseparable friends. To feed him I had to beg scraps from the kitchen. The housekeeper, not being a cat lover, made my task difficult, but I braved her frowns and my cat did not want.

After a time I became suspicious of Black Friar, as his sides began to swell alarmingly, and I noticed he wore a guilty look. Then as weeks passed I realized he was masquerading and was really a female cat, with strong maternal instincts. Before long she produced a family of small Black Friars.

STILL TEACHING

The next class instruction I undertook was a group at the Free Kindergarten Training College, Kew. My pupils were young wholesome girls with motherly instincts.

Having only one term with these first-year students, I knew it was no use teaching the fundamentals of sculpture, nor was I expected to do so. Instead, the girls learnt simply by amusing themselves, expressing how and what they liked and having no restrictions put upon their ambitious aims. I could analyse their characters from their productions for one always portrays oneself in every work. Some produced heavy and laboured efforts whilst others produced dainty and fairy-like sketches. The favourite form of expression was the illustrating of nursery rhymes.

Occasionally a stray cat walked into the studio and was encouraged to pose for the students. For a short time he might act as a perfect model, then finding the job boring, start to clean himself, and when his toilet was completed perhaps crawl on to one of the girls' laps and go to sleep. When refreshed by his siesta he would strut out of the studio with great dignity, leaving students minus a model.

Thinking snails would be more patient sitters, the girls would bring them into the studio and place many of different sizes on the benches. There they would stay in death-like sleep unless a few drops of water were sprinkled on them. This would electrify them into life and they would crawl the whole length of the benches, leaving a silver trail behind. And if a crushing sound was heard it meant that one poor thing had fallen to the floor and met a terrible death.

Then a small child from an adjoining property might climb the fence and gaze through the window. The opportunity of obtaining such a model was not to be missed, for someone was sure to be modelling a child. And so, whilst holding a conversation through the window, the pupil would apply her tool to the already almost completed masterpiece.

"OLA'S LOFT"

After spending three and a half years in a Collins Street studio, I rented a large stable loft in the backyard of a palatial old home in East Melbourne. The top floor was taken up by a groom's room and a large loft. At the foot of a steep stairway was a kitchen and sort of a lobby. Two blocks away I found a suitable studio. Before I managed to settle into my new quarters, I was asked to carry out two rushed commissions so I had to live amongst packing cases for the while. Later I settled into the place that was to be my home for the next three years.

I named my new abode "OLA'S LOFT" and carved in Blackwood a nameplate to be plugged into the wall of the building. My stable loft soon took on the bearing of quaint living quarters, furnished with pieces cadged from my mother's home in Black Rock. I visited her most weekends and generally came home armed with a few treasures, even if only a saucepan or a few odd saucers. I needed saucers badly as I had adopted a fine old lady cat. She was a large tortoiseshell with big appealing eyes. I knew the first time I looked into them that I had to take her to my heart and care for her as only a mother could. At the end of the day when I arrived home from the studio Goldilocks was waiting for me and ready for her dinner. As time passed it became obvious that my stray cat had a lover and so to be in readiness for the coming event, I placed a comfortable box full of woollies in a convenient place in the lobby.

Arriving home from the studio one hot summer evening, my only thought was to rest on the couch for a while before preparing the evening meal. It seemed Goldilocks had the same idea. She followed me up the steep steps and settled on the couch before I could get there. I moved her up to the corner and she curled up on the Centenary Herald, which I meant to keep as a memento as I had been mentioned in the art notes; but after the puss had finished with it the paper was only fit to be burned, for it became obvious that her confinement was imminent. I rushed downstairs to bring up her box and found that she had already given birth to two small daughters, who were the image of herself. The next birth, in which I officiated, was a wee smokey-grey son. By this time the landlord had come to my assistance. We secured another box with nice clean bedding, and in it placed Goldilocks and her three babies. All seemed peaceful and I prepared for bed. I had a last glance at the family, and to my surprise, found it had increased by one. Her last born was a ginger kitten. The two little girls were put to sleep, but Smokey and Ginger were allowed to live for a few days.

The next morning I left the small family in their box in the lobby. When I came home from the studio that evening, a stray Tom cat ran out of the doorway. The next morning there was only the tail left of Smokey and the poor mother puss was carrying Ginger around the yard as if looking for a place to hide her only child. I unlocked the kitchen door and she ran upstairs with her precious burden. After the terrible experience I decided to leave her there and keep her under lock and key whilst I was away.

All went well for a few days and then tragedy occurred. I was dressing to go to a lecture at the University, and had carelessly left the kitchen door open. Soon I heard a commotion, for Goldilocks was putting up a terrific fight. I rushed from my bedroom, only to see old Tom disappearing down the stairs dragging little Ginger by the scruff of the neck. I ran after him, shouting and calling as I went, but the villain disappeared and I never saw him again. My poor cat had lost all her family and I was to blame.

For some days she seemed miserable and kept looking for her lost family. When she recovered, she soon presented me with another ginger kitten. This time I determined that nothing should befall her offspring. They were both kept locked in "OLA'S LOFT" until the baby was old enough to have her freedom.

NEW STUDIO

My new studio was a well built wood-panelled billiard room erected in the back garden of an old terrace house. A glassed in room had been added to the entrance, and as the light was good I did most of my work there. It also served as a temporary home for my next pet, who proved to be quite a personality. I acquired him in an unusual way, and long before it was convenient to cope with a lively bird. He was a piping crow, or our Australian black and white magpie.

I will tell you how it all happened. One afternoon I was sitting in the garden which surrounds the studio. Soon I was joined by one of the tenants of the house, and a visitor who had expressed a wish to meet me. In the course of conversation she mentioned that she had a magpie, and she thought she may have to part with him as he annoyed her husband by sneaking into his studio and getting up to all sorts of mischief. His first offence was mild. He had found the nail tin and scattered the contents in all directions, but his second offence was unforgivable. He had interfered with his masters paint box. The tubes were new and shiny, and the magpie was in his element picking holes in them and squeezing paint in all directions, even on a newly painted landscape. This was an unforgiveable sin, and the artist vowed the bird must be given away.

I quickly remarked I would love to have him, but it was not possible at present as I had no home of my own, and to house a mischievous bird on other people's property might lead to complaints. I was discover was the case; for soon I became owner of the bird. I called him Margu. He was simply dumped on me, and I did not see his owner to protest. One morning I found him outside my studio door covered with wire netting bent into a crude cage-like enclosure keep him from escaping. He was sitting on a perch looking the picture of misery but as soon as I appeared carolled a song of joy. I was surprised to see him there, and quite at a loss to know what do with the bird, so I took him into the glassed-in vestibule and shut the door. Having his freedom, he started to poke round as if looking for something to eat, so I went down to the village and bought some raw meat. Whilst cutting it fine on my carpenter's bench, he seemed to sense it was there, as before I had quite prepared his meal, he hopped up, and started stealing pieces from under my knife. He proved a cheeky fellow, and not at all shy.

After sharing my studio with Margu for a few weeks, I cut the feathers of one of his wings short so that he could not fly, thinking if he did escape he may be attacked by wild species of his kind and so meet a horrible end. After taking this precaution I opened the door each morning and allowed him to strut round the garden. He did enjoy these outings, for as soon as I unlocked the door, he hopped from his perch and out before I could bar his way. He poked his beak into all the holes and crevices in the wooden fence that surrounded the garden; dragging out unsuspecting spiders, and gobbling them up before the poor things were aware. Grubs were a particular delicacy and I found myself hunting for them, instead of attending to my sculpture. This service pleased Margu, and if I sat on a bench to rest, he would immediately come and pull my smock as if say: "You are loafing on your job, come and help me find more grubs." And so I had to obey. Following this intelligent bird, I turned over leaves for him to catch the soft green grub disguised on the lining.

When I became engrossed in my work, Margu took the opportunity to wander further afield. When I discovered my loss, I became most upset and walked round and round the neighbourhood searching for him. I sometimes found it necessary to advertise in the daily paper.

One day an Inspector called to say he had had a complaint against Margu. He had raised his magnificent voice with such shrill lovely notes he had disturbed a man with uneducated taste. And besides, he said, I had no right keep the bird as it was protected. I explained the circumstances in which I acquired Margu, and told the sympathetic Inspector that the bird had its freedom and wandered all day long round the garden. He seemed to understand and told me to try to keep him quiet, but of course that was impossible.

My next disturbance was caused by an unpleasant landlord. He remarked that he had watched Margu dropping the iron plug into the washbasin, and it was covered with cracks. I tried to assure him that the cracks were as ancient as the basin, and they were there long before Margu arrived. It was impossible to argue with him, and so I had to pay for a new basin. When I at last found a suitable property to buy I was not sorry to turn my back on this back garden studio, and unpleasant landlord.

"OLA'S HOME"

My new place was to be called "Ola's Home", and now I am here I hope to live in it until my time is ripe, and I am ready to pass on to a fairyland of Little People, and trusting creatures. At least that is what I hope.

The place I bought was an old Cobb and Co's livery stables in East Melbourne, and not far from my previous abode. It was in a bad state of repair, but I saw the possibilities of turning it into a wonderful home and studio combined. I still live in a hay-loft, and the three stables and large coach house are my studios.

The moving day was a nightmare for I had not only to cope with my personal furniture from the loft, but the heavy sculpture, benches, tools, clay bins etc., from the studio; also the sections of two six foot figures I had nearly completed carving in sand stone. When finished they were to be placed over the portico of the new Royal Hobart Hospital. When all this stuff was safely housed, I had to consider my pets. My aquarium had had three lovely gold fish swimming in it, but, sad to say, a nasty stray cat had fished two out, and when I arrived home one evening, I found them lying dead on the cobble stones outside my lobby. There was still a lonely one left, and he had to be moved very carefully in case he spilled out, and also met a tragic death.

Margu and Ginger were carried in baskets. Margu we caged under the courtyard staircase which had been wired off for the purpose. And Ginger was released upstairs. He immediately crawled under my bed, and there he stayed for hours. When he eventually emerged he sniffed all the furniture, and feeling that the strange loft must be his new home, he ate a big meal and settled down to sleep on his favourite chair.

BUILDING A LILY POND

It took all the pets a little time to become accustomed to their new home, but when they settled down, seemed quite happy. I had bought a few fish to keep the lonesome one company. They grew so quickly that very soon it became necessary to make them a new home.

With bricks and mortar I built a lily pond against a wall in my garden. It was oblong in shape with a two foot double brick margin coated with cement. In the centre I placed a large stone carving representing "Mother Earth" carrying "Man" on her broad shoulders. The group looked well surrounded with water, and bright fish swimming amongst lilies, and water reeds.

On sunny days, Ginger would sit on the ledge and watch the fish darting here and there taking cover under the protection of large leaves.

For years this pond gave me great pleasure, until I found the urchins of the district had discovered it. They came armed with tins in which to catch the fish. No amount of scolding would frighten them away. One cheeky fellow I caught and ducked him in the pond. Later his angry mother came and abused me, and so I had to try other methods. In the end it became necessary to have a pig-wire cover made to fit closely over the water. Even this did not stop the boys.

One lad I chased from the edge of the pond, fell when scaling the garden wall. I followed him into the park opposite and started to give him a lecture, but finding he had cut his leg badly, I took his hand and brought him inside to bathe and bandage his damaged limb This I found had more effect than my worthy lecture, for we have been great friends ever since.

KIDNAPPING MARGU

When I was away for a long weekend, a near tragedy happened. Luckily I decided to come back on the Monday, as it was not a compulsory holiday, and I was expecting some large 7' x 2½' plaster panels back from the caster. I had nineteen of these to model for the new Mutual Life and Citizens' building, Sydney, which was being erected at the time. It had to be a hurried job, and so I felt I should get home. It was well I did, for on arrival I was met by many excited children in my garden and Margu in his cage looking most crestfallen and shaken. It appeared that some naughty boys had taken him, and were taking him away in a sack. The neighbouring children had seen the villains committing the crime, and had run post-haste to break the news. At the gateway they had met the driver who had just delivered one of my panels and was about to drive away. With bated breath the children told him what had happened, and being a gallant soul, without further questioning he chased the thieves, and reclaimed Margu. It took the children a long time to tell all the details, and it was hard to decipher the facts, for in their excitement they all talked at once. I jumped to the conclusion that every child was worthy of a reward, so opening my purse I put in each small hand a coin.

I had made friends with the children of the district, and while my garden was being trenched the boys played bushrangers, shooting with imaginary guns all who passed that way. When the sunken lawn was dug it filled with water, and refused to drain away. The children put on bathers and helped me to bail it out. It was great fun splashing about in the mud. Each time it rained the hole became full of water, and so in the end it had to be filled in, and I had to be content with a level lawn.

Having helped in the early stages of the laying out on my garden, the children felt it their privilege to over-run the place. The girls tap-danced in the big studio, and the boys ran about my garden trampling on my newly planted shrubs. In the end I had to give them the cold shoulder, and get on with the job of getting my home in order.

OPOSSUMS

Each year my garden grew more beautiful. Trees, shrubs, and plants, mostly gifts from friends, were planted in every available space. My garden soon became overgrown, it was just a bower of greenery, a place for fairies to play, birds to build their nests, and possums to jump from tree to tree. There were many of these lovely woolly creatures about, and all were very tame. In the day time they slept in the roofs of terrace houses, but at night they awoke, and made straight for my gum trees. I enticed them on to the courtyard roof by placing slices of bread there. Soon every bit disappeared, and they came to my bedroom window asking for more. A mother with a baby clinging to her back was a constant visitor. She even came and sat on my pillow, and if I was asleep, would jump on to my chest, and wake me up. She was nervous of Ginger, and if he came into the room she sprang to the window shelf and off across the galvanized iron roof, making a loud clattering as she went. One night she was so disturbed, she jumped out without her baby who was on top of the wardrobe at the time. I thought I would not alarm the little one, so turned over and went to sleep. In the early morning hours I was awakened by a disturbance in my half closed cupboard. I got up, lit the light, and opening the door looked amongst my clothes, but could see nothing unusual, so I went back to bed. Soon the noise started again. This time I was determined to locate the trouble. Again looking in my wardrobe I saw my best winter dress heaving as if it was coming to life. There was an unusual bump in one of the sleeves, and the baby opossum was curling round and round trying to make a nest for herself. I found it difficult to dislodge the little ball of fluff, and when I did she jumped from my hands, and out of the window like a shot: I concluded she found her mother, for the next night they were back again.

FEEDING BIRDS

During the day I sprinkled seed and bread crumbs on the court-yard roof. Then watched birds of every description devour them. They scratched so vigorously that in time great patches of paint were worn off, and I had to have the roof repainted. When finished the corrugated iron looked so spick and span, that I did not dare throw any more seed there, instead I chose a spot on the lawn. The scratching still continued, and in no time the lawn bore a bald patch. Now I carry their daily meal into the park opposite and sprinkle it on the lawns.

A FAMILY OF SPARROWS

I had accepted a commission to carve a seven foot figure in lime-stone to be erected in Adelaide, a memorial to the Pioneer Women of South Australia. When the three ton block of stone arrived at "OLA'S HOME", the crane which was to lift the block would not pass under the courtyard entrance. The only thing to do was to remove two sheets of the galvanized iron roof, and through the opening drop the jack of the crane. Fastening this to a strong chain that bound the stone, seven men hauled the gigantic mass into position on a wooden base. There I had work in full view of the street, and in all weather for eighteen months.

When I first saw the three-ton block of lime-stone left for me to carve, I felt it looked a cold, austere shape with sharp, square on its corners roughly-dressed surface. It looked hard and unsympathetic to the little me standing at its base, who had to turn it into the like of a living form. I felt almost afraid to chip away its corners to give it a less uninspiring appearance; but once my hammer started to fall, I lost my fear in the will to achieve.

Day after day, week after week, month after month I worked. During this time I made friends with many small families of sparrows who were born and bred in a hole alongside a rafter of the courtyard roof. When standing on scaffolding carving the head and shoulders of my statue, I was almost parallel with my friends' nest, and could watch them bringing up their badly behaved family. At meal time the youngsters used no restraint in the effort to get all that was offering. Those who opened their mouths widest seemed to get the most. Sometimes their squawking was so disturbing, that I rested my hammer to see what was happening, quite expecting a fight. But, no, it was only a meal! As they grew bigger, their vigour became more noticeable, for they were getting ready to fly. In a few days the nest was empty. My friends had gone, the babies had found wings. I missed them badly, and was glad when a new Spring arrived and I could watch the activities of rebuilding the nest, or repairing the old in preparation for another family. I never lost interest in the sparrows, and even when carving delicate parts of the face, I found time to stop and observe the placing of a twig, and later soft feathers. When all the fuss of nest repairing was over, there was less movement in the corner. The reason was obvious, for on craning my neck I could see the female contentedly sitting on her eggs. It was not until the family hatched that my interest was again aroused by the noisy chicks who were always ready for a feed. They kept their parents busy bringing choice grubs for them to guzzle. With all this packing in of food they soon grew strong and vigorous, and showed impatience to venture into the world. Then one day the entire family flew away, and if it had not been for a dramatic happening I should have never recognised them again.

They had chosen a very unpleasant day to leave home. It was cold with drizzling rain. I was working on my statue under cover of the courtyard roof, and so had a fine view of their departure. For a while I enjoyed the quiet of their empty nest, and continued to chip away at my block of stone, occasionally resting my hammer to watch Margu strutting about the garden, stopping now and again to pounce upon an unsuspecting worm which had come to the surface to enjoy the rain. Suddenly he darted into some shrubs near at hand, and catching a small sparrow by the leg appeared with the poor wee thing flapping and screeching in its effort to free itself.

I lay my tools aside and chased Margu to try and make him drop the bird before he bashed its brains out. But he was very quick, and ran round and round my statue with me in hot pursuit threatening him with the garden broom. My great form and my anger must have frightened him, for suddenly he loosened his grip, the baby sparrow escaped, and scuttled under the base of the stand which carried the three ton block of stone which was in time to become a memorial. At most the space between this base and the pitchers that paved the courtyard was not more than three inches. By laying flat on my tummy I could not get my hand under far enough to reach it, and besides I could not distinguish the bird from the many chips of stone that had collected there. Then I tried scraping under with my chisel, but only succeeded in frightening the sparrow further away, and dislodging a few more stones. My next effort was with a three-foot rule, this method repaid by bringing the bird out plus many stones. Catching the scared little thing, I wondered what on earth I should do with it, as it was getting late and there was no sign of the parents. If only I could reach the nest, and shove it in; thinking it would be more comfortable for it to die in its own home, rather than be killed by Margu or Ginger!

Mounting the ladder, I found by standing precariously on the top rung I could just reach the entrance to the nest. So shoving the little fellow into his deserted home, I descended, and picking up my chisel and hammer started to work in an attempt to race the fading daylight.

The following morning the parent birds discovered their lost child, and started feeding it without delay, flying in and out with choice bits of food. The baby squawked in its excitement, and seemed more lively than ever. Perched on the edge of the nest and flapping its tiny wings as if to fly at any minute. The next time I looked it was sitting between its parents on the clothes line; from there it flew to the garden, and on to the electric light wire, where its parents, brother and sister were all perched in a row, and I could not tell my hero from the other youngsters. They were all so fluffed out and contented looking, that I turned back to my work, letting them enjoy their freedom and fly further afield.

MAKING A CAKE

I had just mixed the ingredients for a cake, and had placed it in the oven when an author friend arrived. She was full of admiration at the tremendous growth of my garden since Franziska had laid it out. "I have some shrubs for you in the car" She said. "Come I will help you plant them". With the thought of the lovely gift, I forgot about the cake I had just placed in the oven for a special guest I expected in the afternoon. We walked down the steps arm in arm, and after planting out the shrubs, sat on a garden seat. From a bag she brought forth a manuscript. "Let me read you part of my latest play", she said. In her deep heavy voice she started, and before she had got very far I realised that she was not only an author, but also an actress for she made me laugh and cry in turn. At the end of the reading, I felt I had been to the theatre, and thoroughly enjoyed myself.

After waving her "Good-bye" I sprinkled crumbs on the lawn, and watched birds devour them. Then turning on the fountain, stood back to let them bathe. They splashed with great glee, and later preened their feathers on the rim of the bird bath like doves on Michelangelo's bowl. The sun was shining brightly, and it was a lovely day.

Sitting on the edge of my fish pond, I seemed to attract the many fish that swim there; for coming to the surface, they welcome me by opening and shutting their mouths as if asking in fish language to be fed. Hurriedly I complied with their wish, and sprinkled some food amongst the lilies. Then the fun began, they splashed and darted here and there in their greedy efforts to swallow as much as possible, making the while a colourful pattern below the surface of the water. For a long time I watched them, then went into the studio, and seeing some unfinished work, commenced to model. Under my touch the clay took shape, and soon an interesting study appeared. Occupied in the effort of my creation I lost all sense of time, but my sense of smell is keen, and soon drifting on the breeze came the smell of burnt cake! I did not sniff twice before I realised what was happening. Dropping my tool, I ran upstairs, and bounding into the kitchen, found it full of blue-black smoke, and fragrance of over-cooking. Quickly turning off the gas I threw wide open the oven door, and peered inside. All that remained of my cake was a small black cinder.

WILLIAM RICKETTS

I had just come home from opening another of William Ricketts' exhibitions in the natural surroundings of his wonderful Mountain Gallery in the beautiful Dandenong Ranges on the outskirts of Melbourne. This was the third time he had honoured me. The other two exhibitions were held in City Halls, and had none of the magical atmosphere of his Sanctuary.

Threatening him with a garden broom

Sitting on the edge of my fish pond

William is a natural modeller. Using cream clay, he powders it with shaded earth from the wayside to get his coloured effects. Quite untrained, he works out his own spiritually inspired salvation; using the Aboriginal mystical myths as his subjects. He has a sense of design, and in some pieces of his sculpture he strikes a dramatic conception that is original and telling. His work is different from the accepted sculpture, but so is William Ricketts different from the average man. A fey atmosphere surrounds him and is portrayed in his work.

The State Government has now taken over his property, and have built him a studio home with kiln and all conveniences. When the time allows he will enrich the building with his works.

For years he has opened his gates to the public, and they wander through his hand-made paths shaded by mountain trees, native shrubs and magnificent tree ferns. Amongst all this wilderness he has placed his work. At every turn and twist of a path there are new surprises awaiting the delighted visitor.

I am never tired of visiting William, and with a basket full of vegetarian food, we enjoy it amongst his half finished statues in the crowded space of his original log hut. Now that he has such a grand new home, I hope he will not discard this old building with its fairy-like atmosphere. Perhaps he will bequeath it to the creatures of his Bushland, for I am sure a new home would not be the same to them.

During our meal we watched William feed his tame Lyre Bird. She strutted into his hut and helped herself to crumbs he scattered on the floor. Out of the doorway were small birds feeding on grated cheese placed on rocks amongst tall tree ferns, and his splendid sculpture. There were some beautiful species hopping from stone to stone. William's supply of cheese never runs out, and as soon as one rock table is cleared of food morsels, another handful is replaced.

In the night, when the light has faded, and William has completed a full day's work, he sits in his old arm-chair and waits for his pet possums to appear so as to share his evening meal with them. When all are satisfied he closes his eyes, and William's soul drifts in sleep to the centre of Australia; there to join his beloved native tribe, in their natural setting. He is so at home with these true Australians, that every year or so he packs his truck and caravan full of clay and tools, and starts on his long journey to the red heart of Australia. For months he lives there with his primitive friends, modelling portraits of the old and young to bring back to his Mountain Gallery, later to be used as models for new inspired conceptions.

BUCHANAN

Much against Mother's wishes a dog had entered the family circle in her Black Rock home. She had previously said she would not have one about the place. Knowing her antipathy, Franziska defied authority, and paying ten shillings for a tiny pup, brought him home in the palm of her hand. He was a pretty little mongrel with great charm of character. Being black and white, my sister named him Buchanan. He seldom got his full name, but answered to Buck, Bucko, Buckey, and Bucket. He was to be well brought up and not allowed inside the house, neither was he to ride in the car; but since he sneaked into both as soon as the doors were open, the restrictions lapsed.

When taken for a walk on the bush-covered cliff over-looking Port Phillip Bay, Buck very soon became tired. He would just sit and refuse to move, knowing that Franziska would pick him up and carry him the rest of the way home. She loved this rugged little dog, and spoiled him accordingly. When she died suddenly before she reached her prime, Buck became a real problem. Mother had to care for him, and this worried her as he would bark and chase cars. His particular enemies were the butcher and the postman. He would sneak up behind them and nip their legs. On one occasion he bit too hard, and mother received a letter from the Postal Department saying that the postman had had hospital treatment, and was claiming damages. This so upset mother, that Marc gave the dog away to a workman who lived in Kangaroo Flat, a small village a few miles from Bendigo, and well over a hundred miles from Black Rock, so that Buck would not return to worry mother.

He did not stay in his new home long. He just disappeared, and not until nine months later when Marc and his wife called on a friend who lived in Kangaroo Flat was he discovered. Hearing their voices, Buck ran out to greet them.

It appeared this little stray dog had been about the village for many weeks, and before that a drover was known to have had him. He had grown thin, dirty, and very miserable, and for one who had always lived in luxury, this form of vagabond existence must have been terrible.

One morning when our friend and her daughter were out shopping they were discussing her daughter's fiancee, whose name was also Buck, when to their astonishment, this pretty, but dirty little stray dog adopted them, and every time they mentioned the name Buck he wagged his tail and became excited. As they walked he followed close to their heels, and when coming to the gate, he stood waiting to be admitted. Instead the gate was closed in his face and he was told to "go home"; but since he had no home, he took no notice, and going round to the back entrance was soon at their heels again with his tail wagging. Persisting with his claim of friendship they felt bound to give him a much needed meal, and to allow him to stay. And stay he did, each day worming his way further into their hearts until he had placed himself firmly there, and come what may, they could not give him up.

SPORTS' SHOP WINDOW

I never tired of my interest in wild creatures; so imagine my distress when one afternoon, whilst shopping in the city, I saw in a sports' shop window, spot-lighted brilliantly, a duck swimming ceaselessly round a small pond. I gazed at it, (I must say without my glasses), and thought the poor bird looked absolutely terrified as it glided over the water and watched the many faces pressed against the window pane, for out of each head gazed two curious eyes. The poor wild creature returned their gaze with a glassy stare. I edged my way through the crowd, and having a closer view decided that the cruelty to this tortured thing should not be tolerated. I hurried away from the shop and stepped abroad the first tram that came along. There I sat in broody silence, and did not awake from my troubled meditation until I found I was on the wrong tram and miles away from East Melbourne.

Arriving home at last, I immediately rang up "The Society for The Protection of Animals", and reported to them what I had just seen. They thanked me kindly, and said they would look into the matter at once. And I felt sure they would, for I had painted a very vivid picture of the cruelty involved. After pouring out the feelings of my heart in the right direction, I felt more contented and as satisfied as a girl guide who had done her good deed for the day.

A week later I was in the city again, and passing the same shop noticed with amazement that the duck was still there, and attracting an audience. I pushed my way to the fore, and I saw the same duck swimming round and round its tiny pond! Fiddling in my hand bag I found my new bi-focal glasses, and placing them on my nose, had an excellent view of the complete layout of the window's display. There were guns and heaps of cartridges on show, and most glorious outfits for the hunter to wear, and gadgets to carry. A cruel setting! Oblivious to its surroundings, the duck swam on in monotonous circles. Its eyes were really set and glassy, its body really stiff and hard. It was a decoy!

"HAD" AGAIN

Soon after this experience, I was "had" again. It happened on my way to a shopping centre to buy a little extra cat's meat as the Monday was a public holiday. On passing a low wall that edged a garden, there was a group of snails. At a quick glance, they appeared half squashed. As each step carried me further on my way, my conscience smote me, for I felt, "the poor things may be in pain, and taking a long time to die!" After walking to the end of the block, I retraced my steps, determined to put an end to their agonies.

Placing my glasses on my nose, I looked closer at the snails and discovered that they were not suffering, but appeared to be gormandising in a cannibal-like fashion on a crushed one of their kind.

SYBIL THORNDYKE VISITS THE STUDIO

I have willed my property to the Melbourne Society of Women Painters and Sculptors. It is already their headquarters, a place where they hold their meetings, lectures, or receive invited celebrities.

On the occasion Sybil Thorndyke visited "Ola's Home" to meet the artists, the Office Bearers had the privilege of meeting her at the gateway.

I, being the President, was to the fore. She shook me warmly by the hand, and before the others had the same privilege; she spotted Ginger sunning himself on the lawn. "Oh, the beautiful cat!" she cried, as she rushed forward and took him in her arms.

From that moment formality ended. She was overcome by my stately cat and all interest was focused on him. Ginger held her whole attention, whilst we took a "back seat", as she cuddled the heavy creature, and he purred loudly. With him clenched in her arms, she entered the Working Studio still caressing him fondly. Margu's anger was immediately aroused, as he was intensely jealous of Ginger. He kept on calling in loud, shrill notes, and went through one song after another. Ginger struggled and escaped, as Sybil stood spell-bound. Coming back to normal, she joined in Margu's song, and together they sang. The louder she raised her lovely voice, the more he harmonized. This fine duet went on for some time, and not until we passed through the little studio into the big one, did Margu stop trying to delay her.

And so the afternoon party was a great success for Ginger and Margu, and of course, for we artists.

THE FAIRY PRINCE

Both my pets were very spoiled, and much to the fore in my home. Ginger had grown to be a very large cat, and was also a very lazy one. He spent most of his time sleeping and eating. Margu was the reverse and was always busy doing something he had no right to do. My nail tin became his play box, and picking out one by one he would throw them on to the floor below, then cock his head to one side, and look down to see where they had fallen. If I picked them up and forgot to move the tin from my bench he would repeat the performance, much as a baby throwing his toys from a pram.

When building a rockery round a cement statue of a fairy imp at the foot of the courtyard stairs, Ginger and Margu seemed to want to help. If I picked Ginger up for a nurse, Margu became pugnacious and aggressive, ready to fight even his own shadow. In these moods he made Ginger's life unbearable, chasing and pecking his tail. On one of these aggressive occasions he got more than he deserved, as Ginger hit back and caught him in the than eye, leaving a nasty scratch near the iris. For a time I thought he would lose his sight; but after spending a week in his cage, with his eye closed, looking most crestfallen, he emerged again cured and chirpy.

After having my house painted I had to call in a Vet to attend to Margu as he had become very sick and had developed a nasty cough. I thought perhaps he had paint poisoning; but the Vet said "No", after examining him, and looking down his throat. During the examining Margu squawked and struggled, and made a tremendous fuss. He soon recovered from his illness; but retained his cough, and used it when he wanted to draw attention.

One morning I was distressed to find Margu lying prostrated at the foot of his cage. I picked the little fellow up and laid him on a soft cushion on a studio chair, and sat mourning over him. In this down-cast attitude I was disturbed by a stranger, who had come begging alms. With tears in his eyes he told me he was a surgeon dentist, and was very ill and could not work. His wife whom he loved very dearly was dying of cancer, and their only child was a soldier lost in New Guinea during war. To hear all this disturbing story in the midst of my sorrow, touched my soft heart.

At my feet lay my dying bird. The stranger stooped and picked him up, and after examining him expressed his verdict. "He has crop binding and needs a dose of castor oil to relieve him." Immediately my heart thumped with hope; and I ran upstairs and got an eye dropper, and between us Margu was given a dose. Then turning to the stranger I handed him a pound note, saying, "Keep this as your fee." After that he left, but was back next morning to inquire for the sick one, and also to sting me for more money. By this time Margu was on his feet, and although very wobbly, he was certainly on the way to recovery. Each day the stranger appeared and begged more money, and in a short time he had wangled quite a lot from me. As time went on I became suspicious of his sincerity, and concluded I was a simpleton.

After his first visit I was so impressed with the miracle of Margu's recovery that I wrote this fairy story whilst squatting Buddha-fashion on the stone seat on my garden with Ginger sitting beside me to keep me company. I called the fantasy "THE FAIRY PRINCE".

"One morning a Fairy Godmother sat quietly meditating at the window of her Castle. On her fingers she counted her many God-children, and finding none of them in want, her conscience was clear. Far below lay a carpet of golden leaves, blown there by the autumn winds. As she watched, more drifted to earth like tears of the giant Poplar trees that stood sentinel at the entrance to her courtyard."

"Slipping on her golden shoes she rose, and standing erect glided from room to room, as if born on the wings of Mercury. Then leaving the castle she descended the steps to the courtyard. There stood her maid as if in great sorrow: In her hands she held the form of a magpie. "He is dying," she sobbed, and laying him on a soft bed of leaves in the cloisters she wrung her hands. Her mistress knelt beside her bird and prayed, long and earnestly, and as she prayed, into her courtyard limped a Fairy Prince in the disguise of a beggar. His tears mingled with those of the Fairy Godmother, and dropping on to the dying bird quickened him back to life. As if with magic power the bird raised himself, and throwing back his head carolled forth a song of joy."

PLANTING A LAWN

As my trees grew the lawn deteriorated, and after a hot summer there was very little grass left. It was only a small square patch with a birdbath in the centre, so I decided the only sensible thing to do was to get my gardener to dig it up and add some new soil. When he had finished his job I came to the fore with a large packet of grass seeds. These I spread over the entire patch, and the gardener covered them with earth,

Building a Rockery

I wrote a fairy tale

and completed the job with a thorough sprinkling from the hose. Well satisfied I went upstairs and busied myself with other jobs.

Later when my gardener had left I walked to my window to admire our handiwork, when to my horror I saw dozens of sparrows and doves having a wonderful time scratching over the soft earth and devouring the seeds.

After a week or so a few patches of grass appeared, but not enough to make a lawn. A friend seeing my disappointment, took pity on me and arrived one day with a carton of Buffalo grass. After she left I got down on my knees and planted it out, watered it and sat back on a garden seat to rest. Margu, who had been in a corner of the garden catching spiders showed no interest in the planting-out procedure until it was all finished. Then he came forward and uprooted every plant, I was very angry and scolded him. He retaliated by screeching and pecking at me with his sharp beak, so I closed him in the studio, whilst I replanted the lawn.

I knew I must protect it in some way, so cut a number of staves and hammered them into the lawn at intervals, then twisted string from one to another, thus making a barricade against Margu. Then I let him out and went upstairs. For some days he behaved very well, but it did not last long. And then one morning I heard a terrific screeching in the garden. It was not the usual noise he made when angry, but held a distressed note. I rushed to his help and found Margu wound in the entanglement. It took me quite a time to cut him free from the string. He must have turned round and round in his fright, and wound himself up like a mummy. When freed, he seemed very shakened. It must have been a lesson to him for although I discarded all the string, he steered well clear of the staves and allowed the lawn to flourish.

A YOUNG VISITING MAGPIE

Margu had had his wing clipped when he came to me, and I did not allow it to grow, as I knew that if he flew away after being so many years in captivity, he would be attacked by wild birds and perhaps meet a distressing death. If magpies flew into my garden he called out to attract my attention. When I went to his rescue he ran quickly, and stood at my feet, and from that safe position screeched at the top of his voice as if to say - "This is my home. You keep away!"

Margu was ageing, and his feet were crippled through many mishaps, but he still was an old warrior with plenty of spirit.

A YOUNG MAGPIE

When a young magpie who had not yet his adult feathers adopted me, Margu accepted him with indifference, but at times seemed to be almost hostile to the newcomer. I first noticed the stray having a bath in Margu's clam shell. Margu was standing a few yards away, and calling loudly for help. I was amused at the antics of the newcomer who was quite oblivious of the liberty he was taking, and flapped away as if in his private swimming pool. When he had finished his toilet, I fed him with finely cut-up meat. This he relished for he seemed very hungry.

Each morning my new friend called from the courtyard roof, and I answered it by throwing him his breakfast. This went on for some weeks. Being thoroughly acquainted, he became more cheeky and even ventured into the studio. On these occasions he took possession of Margu's bench, and hopped on to his perch. To my astonishment Margu allowed this intrusion and the stray became a regular visitor to the studio. I think Margu liked his company, which led me to summarise that perhaps he was in truth a she, and so I named her Perky Miss. I grew quite fond of this wild, half tame creature, and hoped to keep her in that state. I found myself expecting Perky Miss each morning at regular times, and she seldom disappointed me. After she had eaten a goodly portion of Margu's meat, she started to explore the three studios, leaving white spots wherever she went. Her favourite perch was on the heads of my student copies from antique casts. These were rather grubby from the years they had stood on a high shelf, and after the young magpie had used them as a perch they looked rather disgraceful streaked with droppings.

In the late afternoon she left the studio and flew to the park opposite. She eventually had her own sleeping quarters. One morning she did not appear as usual. I was worried and decided that something drastic must have occurred; either she had been killed by a cat, a car, or captured and kept in captivity.

After she had been missing for three months, Perky Miss was brought back by a neighbour who had found her on the door mat, squeaking in a pathetic baby voice as if asking to be let in.

I was glad to see my little friend again, and took her in my arms. She looked neglected; her wing had been cut, and tied to one foot was a length of string. It was matted with black grease from her leg, and the only way to get it off was to cut it away with a razor blade.

Released, she hopped on to Margu's perch, after devouring all his meat.

54

With a cut wing, I knew I had to keep and protect her until she could fly again, and then she could have her freedom. Being wayward, she was not content to live within bounds, and as soon as my back was turned, she would hop onto the garden wall, and over into the lane, and in a few minutes disappear. I found this a great interruption to my work, as I had to spend most of the day wandering round the streets looking for her, I could not control her wayward habit, so in despair, gave her to the Zoo, there to live with many of her kind.

GINGER IN DISTRESS

Ginger seldom caused trouble, although he had the habit of disappearing for a while, then turning up from some mysterious hiding place close at hand. But this did not always happen, and I remember one very harrowing experience after spending a weekend at my mother's home at Black Rock. On returning to "Ola's Home" I found Ginger missing. I called and called; but he did not appear. I had noticed with alarm that his saucers were still full of untouched dried-up meat. The plates were all standing neatly in a row, where the unconcerned tenants of Flat 2 had left them. They obliged me by putting the meat out, but being two young girls of rather frivolous nature were not worried when Ginger did not appear to devour it.

I felt really alarmed, and started a systematic search - but in vain. Where on earth could he be? I thought I could hear a I faint cry coming from somewhere, but could not trace its origin. Three times I went into the yard of the flats next door. My many trips disturbed the tenants, and they joined in the search. They also were able to hear the faint mysterious cry of a cat. It sounded like a voice from the heavens. Looking up we discovered him on the highest part of their roof, so high that it looked almost impossible to rescue him. Going to the front of the building, I saw a long extension ladder leaning against the wall of the adjoining house. It was obvious that he had reached the roof by means of this ladder; and, getting there, had not been able to find his way down again.

In despair I tried to mount the ladder, but being a hefty lass, I became nervous after climbing a few rungs, and so descended. A youth passing came to the rescue and offered his assistance. He climbed the ladder with great vigour, putting me to shame. At this critical moment the owner of the terrace house next door came rushing out of her door. She yelled at the boy - "Come down from there at once, and don't you dare put a foot on my roof! I have just paid to have new tiles laid!" With that announcement she went inside and slammed the door; she obviously was not interested in my poor cat's plight. If she had only given me a word of encouragement, it would have helped a lot. But, no, she slammed the door in my face and left me lamenting and the lad too nervous to proceed any further. At this critical point, inspiration came whispering in my ear, and led me in the direction of the local Police Station, which was only a few yards away. There I enlisted the help of a young, handsome policeman, who on hearing my sad story, picked up his helmet, and followed me. He scaled the ladder easily, and climbing the roof without damaging the tiles, he had no trouble in catching Ginger, who climbed straight into his arms, so glad was he to make contact with a human being after spending two days on the exposed roof during a heat wave with a temperature in the nineties.

As soon as this handsome hero of mine had Ginger in his arms, he started to descend the tall ladder. All went well until he got half way down. At this perilous position, Ginger started to struggle, and being a powerful cat it was all the policeman could do to hold him. I was afraid he would escape, and in his fear climb the ladder again; so I started calling in endearing terms - "It's alright Ginney darling, don't be frightened! You'll be down soon." This outburst of feelings on my part drew a large audience who were obviously amused, but I was oblivious to them; my only concern being the welfare of my cat. Soon he was in my arms, and after the dramatic rescue seemed timid and shaken, so I hurried home to comfort and feed him.

SMOKEY

After I had lived in "OLA'S HOME" for some years, a young half-Persian cat adopted me. I felt that one cat was enough, so gave him away to Steve, a workman who was doing some repairs to the house at the time. He lived in a slum district, and all the alley Tom cats gave poor little Smokey an awful battering. Then he developed an ulcer on his leg. Steve was very distressed about the matter, and so I decided the only thing to do was to take him back and get a Vet's advice. The change of homes had made him very nervous, and it was a long time before he became normal; but when he did, he seemed to take possession of the house. He rather liked Ginger, and for that reason my heart softened towards him. Smokey was a smooger, and looked to his own comfort. If Ginger was on my seat, and for that reason I had to take another, Smokey would join him and then start cleaning his pal's face with enthusiastic licks, and at the same time gradually working himself into the back position near the cushion and into a warmer place in which to go to sleep. Seeing the two of them curled up for the night, I decided to go to my own bed and do the same.

A TRIP ABROAD

In the morning I awoke with the idea of taking another trip abroad. I was naturally anxious about leaving my pets behind, so I set about getting a capable housekeeper to look after them and my garden. At this time Ginger was sixteen years old and Margu perhaps a little older, but as the Vet assured me that they and Smokey were in good health, I felt safe going for a prolonged holiday. And so in 1950 I spent a crowded thirteen months away from Australia.

London can always hold my interest, and I can generally discover something new to me. My first impression on seeing it after the war was how little the surface had changed since my student days; but that was only a fleeting idea, for I found many ugly gaps and charred burnt-out buildings. Although there was so much devastation, it was surprising how little of the really interesting places were destroyed; or else they were patched up in such a way that I was not conscious of the damage that had been done. Churches were badly hit, and many merely shells; amidst all this devastation St. Paul's Cathedral towered like a lonely austere sanctuary. The atmosphere round this great building was grim, but I could see the soul of London still living on, as if her battered hide could "Take it."

Amongst the ruins crept neglected looking cats. Hoping to make them feel a little happier, I brought a couple of pounds of cut-up meat and threw it to the poor creatures, who quickly devoured my offerings.

CAMPING IN A FRIEND'S STUDIO

I camped in a friend's studio during my stay, and made it my headquarters. When I wandered on the Continent, or as far afield as Iceland, I always had a home in Putney waiting for my return. In between these trips I could not resist ordering a hundredweight of clay, and building up a few compositions which I had cast in bronze to bring back to Australia.

This enthusiastic modelling inspiration occurred during the coldest days of the English winter. It was too damp to venture out so sitting in front of the fire, I entertained myself with clay and tools. When my hands got too cold to work any longer, I lay on my bed covered with a rug. One afternoon when I had only just closed my eyes I saw a vision of my lovely Ginger lying on a cushion. He was curled up as if asleep. But I knew immediately that his beautiful body was stiff and cold. His soul had passed on.

For days I wondered and worried, and blamed myself for leaving him to die without my comfort. One day a letter came from my brother - Ginger had passed on.

Whilst in England leading a carefree life, doing just the things I wanted to do, seemed at the time the only life I knew. I thought I would never settle down on my return, nor would I be content with my old life. But when I got home I felt I knew no other life. My trip was just a dream, and now being awake, I enjoyed it, for I was home.

I ADOPT RUFUS

Shortly before I left for England I made friends with a little girl at one of my big studio doors which opens on to a back street. In her arms she held a wee kitten of a few weeks old. It was a firey red and white. I was given a short cuddle, and on returning it to its owner, she skipped away with it in her arms.

When I arrived back in Australia a year later, the kitten had grown into a gawky long-legged cat. It was very neglected, and seemed to sleep in a dilapidated car parked outside my big studio door. I carried scraps of meat to it, and very soon it became my friend, and lived more in "OLA'S HOME" than in its own, he was always in the kitchen when I was preparing Margu's and Smokey's meal. It took its place in my home as if it belonged, so I asked its owner if she wanted the cat, and if not, could I have it. She replied, "You had better keep it. My son won't allow it in the house." The remark was enough for me. I there and then decided to adopt my thin, long-legged friend, and called him Rufus. With good feedings and Smokey as a companion, he grew fat, lazy, and very happy.

Smokey took kindly to his adopted brother, treating him in the friendly manner as he did Ginger by licking Rufus's face clean whilst gradually working his way into the warmest corner of my chair with poor Rufus on the outside to keep him warm. And so throughout their lives they remained the best of friends, and I had to sacrifice my seat.

CATS' CEMETERY

Shortly after I came back from England, Smokey's health began to fail; and, although he lived for a few years, it became necessary, later, to have him put to sleep. I buried him beside other pets in a plot of ground at the foot of a large stone carving of "Mother Earth" with Man, symbolized as a child, firmly seated on her shoulder.

I carved the group whilst a student in London, and brought it back to Australia. When Franziska, who was a landscape gardener, planned my garden, she used the group as a centre piece to the lily pond.

I enjoyed the pleasure of this pond for many years until it started to leak, and then it gave me endless trouble. In despair I housed the fish in a large aquarium, and filled in the pond with garden soil, and planted colourful shrubs.

I called the plot the "Pets' Cemetery," for my much loved creatures, and later for my own ashes. As each one dies, I carve a white marble headstone bearing the deceased's name.

SOUTER TURNS UP

Rufus missed Smokey, and seemed very lonely, so I was glad when a black and white cat dropped in one day to visit us. He was always in the kitchen at meal time, and later curled up in the middle of my tenant's bed. At night he gave her little room to turn, but not wishing to disturb him, Ada put up with much discomfort.

We called him Souter after the Sydney "Bulletin" artist who was well known for his excellent drawings of black and white cats. Souter is still with us, although Rufus now lies beside Smokey at the foot of the monument.

MARGU AT REST

Margu has now passed on after living twenty seven years in my care. No longer does the studio ring with his lovely voice. Nor are my friends entertained by his antics. For he was always up to mischief, and when backs were turned would help himself to our afternoon tea by picking great holes in a freshly baked cake, or disturbing our quiet by throwing all the tea spoons on the ground. All this naughtiness was done in the "twinkling of an eye" whilst my friends were trying out their skill with clay from the bin.

When chased away, he vented his anger on the door mat, attacking it furiously and calling at the top of his shrill voice whilst pulling out great lumps of matting. After satisfying his wrath, he strutted into the garden to hunt for spiders. All this fun is now in the past, and Margu's soul now wanders with my other pets in an animal Paradise, where I shall join them later.

WE NAMED HER KATIE

I only had Souter left, and decided I would not have another cat, unless, of course, it was a ginger or a smokey-grey. In a weak moment I gave vent to my thoughts, and, a friend being in ear shot made a mental note of the fact. It was not long before she turned up with a wee, half Persian, smokey-grey and white kitten which she assured me was a male. It was only a few weeks old and had not yet learned to lap milk. I had to feed it with an eye dropper. When its "tummy" was firm and bloated with milk, I lay it in my cat's basket and closed the lid.

During the night I placed the kitten's cot on the foot of my bed and tried to go to sleep, but its pitiful cries kept me awake most of the night, and knowing that it must be hungry, I had to get up and warm more milk.

Soon it learnt to squeeze out of the air-rung spaces round the top of the basket and creep into bed with me. It seemed to give it comfort and warmth, for it lay in the crest of my arm, and sucked the sleeve of my nightgown. There we slept together and our nights were more comfortable. When it learnt to lap milk from a saucer, my anxiety was lessened, for to be a foster-mother to so young a kitten can be very trying.

One sad day the kitten disappeared. Every cupboard and corner of the house was searched and as it was only a few weeks old and quite unable to fend for itself, I felt desperately worried for its welfare. Just as I was giving up all hope of seeing the little creature again, some friends arrived and they all joined in the search. They looked in all the places I had been through again and again, and of course it was not there. When Barrie suggested we pull back the bedclothes in case the wee thing might be hiding there, I pooh poohed the idea as no lump was visible. But Barrie persisting, drew back the bedclothes and there it was, fast asleep nestled between the pillows of my double bed. When disturbed the kitten yawned, stretched, and then settled back to sleep again. We let it be and went down to the studio and commenced to work at our various conceptions.

When a little older the kitten loved to hinder me when bed-making by climbing up the clothes, and as I threw a blanket over would play beneath, making a moving lump that travelled from one side to the other. Always in a hurry to get down to the studio, I left it to find its own way out, which it did most successfully as soon as I left the room, and was at my heels, afraid it might miss some adventure.

Ada and I learnt to love this little ball of fluff, and when we discovered it was a female, nothing on earth would make us part with her. After an operation, we named her Kitty, then Katie, but she was seldom called anything but "The Little-ee."

She grew more beautiful every day, and developed a wonderful tail which she held high with such dignity that one would have thought her father was a squirrel, or perhaps a ferret; for her body grew long, but her legs remained short like all well bred Persian cats. All these qualities turned her into a most elegant looking creature, and really much too beautiful for a male.

Although she is nearly two years old, she still considers me her mother and Ada her foster-mother. She takes her best chair, and poor Ada has to sit on another; but when her tummy is empty she comes to me.

NOW SAMUEL

At the end of each year I badly need a holiday, so leaving my pets in the care of Ada, my artist friend Kit, and Barrie who lives next door, I disappear for a month to my beloved Cowes.

Whilst on a recent visit, I met a Professor who had a huge ginger cat he unfortunately had to keep in a cage at the University, and wanted to find a home for him. I felt instantly I must rescue that cat from its small enclosure and give him his freedom. I will never be sorry for my decision. He proved to be a magnificent cat with a most lovable nature. I named him Samuel, or The Big Boy. Now he takes Ada's best seat. Katie has to be content with her guest's chair, whilst Ada is forced to sit on an upright one.

Although we all love our new pet, Souter strongly objects to him, and on no terms will he make friends. Instead of sleeping in Ada's room, stretched out by the fire, or on her bed, he prefers to go next door to Barrie's flat, and has adopted her, only appearing in "OLA'S HOME" at meal time.

If it is cold and Barrie is home, he presents himself early in the day, announcing his arrival by jumping at the door with such force that it rattles on its hinges. When let in he makes straight for the most comfortable chair and as near the gas fire as possible, until time for his evening meal, when he deigns to visit me.

He eats contentedly with the other cats, although keeping as far from Samuel as possible, for the Big Boy, now feeling established in the home, objects to Souter's periodical appearances. So to keep the peace, I have to place their dishes far apart.

CREATURES HAVE A DEFINITE COLOUR SENSE

I have noticed through my long association with creatures that they have a definite colour sense. Magpies and Pee-Wees are generally seen together. Both being black and white seems to make them akin. Although Margu had a dislike for cats and always flew at them, pecking them hard and making them run, he seemed to quite like Souter and accepted him as a pal because of their similar colouring.

Souter not only dislikes Samuel but he also dislikes his colouring, and when strolling on the top shelf of Barrie's book-case, he spied a yellow china cat amongst the ornaments, put out his paw and knocked it off. Three times Barrie has found the little yellow cat under the sofa.

SOUTER GOES EXPLORING

One day a roll of new carpet arrived for the flat's hall and was left not very far from Barrie's door. Souter must have thought it was a rabbit burrow and worth exploring. When Barrie saw him disappearing inside it, she held her breath, thinking he may get stuck half way. But no, soon his cheeky head appeared at the far end. He thought it was fun, so repeated the performance.

When let out he wanders round the neighbourhood, paying visits to his many friends in other flats. When his strenuous day is over, he again calls on his good friend Barrie to sleep it off. By this time Barrie has generally retired and is sound asleep, dreaming of fairy folk, and is rudely disturbed by the ruffian thumping at her door, and in between thumps meowing in a raucous voice. Then more thumps and more raucous cries, until in the end he not only wakes Barrie, but the folk in the flat opposite. Coming back from dreamland, Barrie rubs her eyes, and slipping on her dressing gown opens the door to Souter. Although she scolds him for disturbing her slumbers, he takes no notice of her abuse and walking straight to her bed settles down in the warmest spot in the middle, leaving hardly enough room for Barrie to squeeze in. And so they sleep like "Babes in the Wood" until the early hours of the morning, when again he sees fit to disturb her slumbers, and asks to be let out.

TOPSY ARRIVES

Topsy (for she is as black as coal) has just entered our family circle. Where she came from no one knows for her ways and manners are obviously those of a pet who had once lived in a friendly home. Did she belong to someone who had changed address and left her behind? Or perhaps she had wandered back from her new home not liking the surroundings!

For months she lived in the hall of the flats next door, begging food and friendship from all who passed her by and creeping into their flats for a cuddle or warm by their fire, but when the night came she was turned out to wander - so you see Topsy had no real home.

What happened in those "Walk-abouts" no one knows, for one morning she appeared in great distress. The Vet said she had been hit or knocked very hard on the side of her head, and it had left her with a permanent list. Being "fed up" with having no definite home, she wandered in here, and the other three cats accepted her.

AN OASIS FOR BIRDS CATS AND FAIRIES

Coping with my cats and their little idiosyncrasies needs a very patient nature, for I never know what to expect next. Souter will not give up his wandering ways; Samuel refuses to take exercise and sleeps most of the day; whilst little Katie uses my furniture and new carpet on which to sharpen her claws, which causes me concern. But with all their faults, I love them for what they are.

My garden is an oasis for birds, cats and fairies. Although the two former do not agree and I often have had to release a feathered friend from the jaws of my naughty cats, the birds still continue to frequent my garden, and I hope they always will.

I sometimes say firmly "I will not have another pet," but still they continue to stray into "OLA'S HOME", and, looking into my face, seem to say "I have come to stay" - and of course they do!

THE END

www.ingramcontent.com/pod-product-compliance
Lightning Source LLC
Chambersburg PA
CBHW081552040426
42448CB00016B/3300